STEAM AND THE SEA

PAUL FORSYTHE JOHNSTON

With the author's compliments —

Paul F. Johnston

Peabody Museum of Salem   Salem, Massachusetts   1983

Library of Congress Cataloging in Publication Data

Peabody Museum of Salem.
    Steam and the sea.
    Bibliography: p.
    Includes index.
    1. Steam-navigation—History—Exhibitions. 2. Steamboats—History—Exhibitions.
3. Peabody Museum of Salem—Catalogs. I. Johnston, Paul Forsythe, 1950-   . II. Title.
VM605.P38 1983   387.2′4′07401445   83-19451
(Paper) ISBN 0-87577-073-8   (Hardbound) ISBN 0-87577-074-6

Front cover illustration is a detail from an oil painting by Samuel Walters depicting the departure from England of Jenny Lind, August 1850.

Back cover illustration: ticket for the steamboat *Massachusetts*, 1817.

Designed by David Ford
Typeset by DEKR Corporation
Printed by Meridian Printing
Manufactured in the United States of America

CONTENTS

ACKNOWLEDGMENTS

Steam and the Sea was produced to accompany a special exhibition by the same name opening at the Peabody Museum in October 1983. A number of individuals and institutions provided assistance in the preparation of this project, and it is a pleasure to have this opportunity to acknowledge that aid and its sources.

The exhibition, catalog and related programs were funded in part by the National Endowment for the Humanities, the Nimrod Press, Boston, and the Peabody Museum.

Materials for the exhibition were provided by several institutions, including the Francis Russell Hart Nautical Museum of the Massachusetts Institute of Technology, Cambridge, The Library of Congress, Washington, The Marine Museum at Fall River, Inc., The Mark Twain Memorial, Hartford, and The Smithsonian Institution, Washington. John Waterhouse, Curator of the Hart Nautical Museum and John Gosson, Curator of the Marine Museum at Fall River were especially helpful and generous both with their advice as well as their respective museums' collections.

Exhibition materials from the collections of Bell Laboratories, Peter Gimbel and Elga Andersen of The Doria Project, William H. Guild, James Pettee, Mr. and Mrs. Richard W. Pratt, Ruth Robinson, Tracy G. Thurber, and an anonymous donor are also most gratefully acknowledged.

Technical research and graphic interpretation were provided by Worcester Polytechnic Institute students Carol E. Clark, Laurie A. Cocchi and John W. McNeil under the supervision of Professors E. Malcolm Parkinson and John P. van Alstyne. Research and collections preparation were furnished by Peabody Museum volunteers Durland Brown, Laurence B. Brown, Kenneth G. Cady, Chieko Conrad, Hilton Fisher, William P. Hunnewell, Frederic B. Mayo, Gilbert R. Payson, Howard B. Sprague and Frank Watson. John C. Bower, Jr., E. Kenneth Haviland and Francis Lee Higginson, Jr. provided much-needed editorial assistance, and curatorial intern Janine E. Skerry was also most helpful throughout every phase of the project. I am also greatly indebted to the administrative, curatorial, educational and exhibition production staff of the Peabody Museum for the preparation and coordination of the various elements of *Steam and the Sea*.

Acknowledgments

Special thanks are due to Sargent Bradlee for his longstanding interest in the steamship collections donated by his uncle, Francis B. C. Bradlee, over the course of many years' association with the museum. Finally, the Peabody Museum owes a particular debt of gratitude to Francis Lee Higginson, Jr., without whose enthusiasm, encouragement and support this undertaking would not have been possible. It is to him that this work is most gratefully and respectfully dedicated.

October 1983   Paul Forsythe Johnston, Ph.D.

Curator of Maritime History

1 / THE IMPACT OF THE STEAMSHIP

Commercial engine-powered ships are the largest moving objects ever designed by man. In today's world, with its jetliners transporting passengers across the Atlantic in less than four hours and rapid transit "bullet" trains capable of 160 miles per hour in daily use in Europe and the Orient, it is difficult to understand or even imagine the immense and far-reaching impact of the commercial steamship upon worldwide cultural and technological development, from its earliest practical application in the early nineteenth century right through to the present.

During the first quarter of the nineteenth century, the steamboat was little more than a novelty. The vast majority of waterborne trade was carried aboard sailing vessels of all sizes and types. Throughout history, however, sailing ships have been wholly dependent upon the vagaries of wind and weather for the scheduling of arrivals and departures. Heavy weather or calms might delay a voyage for days or even weeks, with the ship idle and the bills mounting. Under such conditions, for example, a transatlantic crossing by a sailing vessel in the late nineteenth century might take anywhere from four to eight weeks. However, with their greater speed and maneuverability, and less reliance upon the elements, even the earliest transatlantic steamers in the 1830s could travel between the Old and New Worlds in no more than eighteen days. By the end of the nineteenth century, the great Blue Riband steamers regularly crossed the Atlantic in a fraction over five days; by the early 1950s, this figure was reduced even further, to slightly more than three days. The progressively briefer and more reliable passages, resulting from rapidly improving engine and hull design and intense competition among the major steamship companies, permitted increasingly lower rates and fares, and far more efficient transportation of goods and people along the world's major trading routes than had been possible aboard sailing vessels. By 1875, the end of the Great Age of Sail, which had dominated the world's waterways for more than four thousand years, was well in sight.

The same factors that caused the steamship to replace the sailing vessel

This mid-nineteenth century oil painting by J. G. Evans and E. Arnold of the steam tug *Panther* towing the ships *Shirley* and *Julius* demonstrates the greater power and maneuverability of the steam-powered vessel over the sailing ship (M-1962, Courtesy of the Essex Institute).

Cunard Line poster, ca. 1914, of the last great four-funnel passenger liner ever built, the *Aquitania* (M-11214, F. B. C. Bradlee Collection).

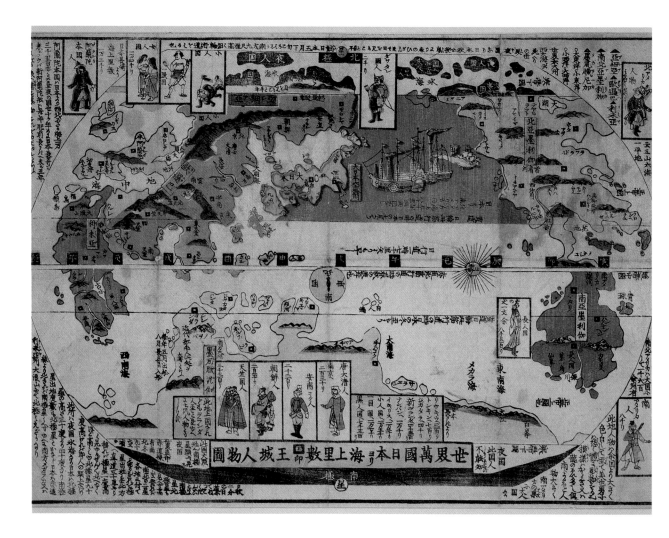

Mid-nineteenth century Japanese print illustrating Commodore Matthew Perry's journey across the Pacific to Japan in 1853. This historic steamship voyage resulted in the inauguration of diplomatic relations between Japan and the West (M-13282A, Francis B. Lothrop Collection).

along the major waterways also promoted widespread travel and sightseeing. The institution of frequent and regular sailing schedules, and the proliferation of steamship companies from the mid-nineteenth century onward, opened the European and American continents to extensive tourism from within and outside their own borders. Expansive advertising campaigns undertaken by the major steamship companies competing among themselves for the tourist trade gradually made the overseas voyage as integral a part of the traveller's experience as the subsequent overland journey. The increased contact among geographically and ethnically diversified cultures resulted in the widespread dissemination of literary, artistic, architectural

PUBLISHED BY CURRIER & IVES   125 NASSAU ST. NEW YORK

THE GREAT MISSISSIPPI STEAMBOAT RACE.
FROM NEW ORLEANS TO ST. LOUIS, JULY 1870.

The Boats left the Wharf at New Orleans, June 30th 1870 at 4.55 P.M. The Lee reached the Wharf Boat at St. Louis July 4th at 11.25 A.M.

Between the R.E.Lee, Capt. John W. Cannon and Natchez Capt. Leathers. WON BY THE R.E.LEE, TIME:3 DAYS 18 HOURS AND 30 MINUTES; DISTANCE 1210 MILES.

The Natchez reached the Wharf Boat at St. Louis, July 4th at 5.58 P.M. six hours & thirty-three min. behind the Lee, having been detained six hrs by a Fog at Devils Id

and cultural tastes and styles. Not only did the steamship hasten these pro-cesses and make them available to a broader segment of the general popula-tion, but it also itself served as a major thematic element of nineteenth cen-tury European and American art, literature, speech and song. In the field of literature, for example, among the works of Joseph Conrad, Charles Dick-ens, Edna Ferber, Jack London, Herman Melville, Eugene O'Neill, Robert Louis Stevenson and Mark Twain, the steamship served such diverse roles as a symbol for the contemporary pride and progress in technology, a meta-phor for the conflict between man and nature, and as an element of plot and setting. The Mississippi riverboat, second only to the cowboy as the quin-

Popular Currier & Ives print, ca. 1870, of the most famous steam-boat race ever held. The *Natchez*, which lost, is shown "holding the horns" on the deckhouse roof. During the actual race, the two vessels were never in sight of one another (M-12712, Gift of Julia M. Fairbanks).

Two pieces of sheet music commemorating Cyrus W. Field and the laying of the first transatlantic telegraphic cable in 1858 (Phillips Library, Driscoll Collection).

tessential American product, achieved such international popularity that wagers were placed as far away as Berlin and Vienna on the outcome of the famous race down the Mississippi between the *Natchez* and the *Robert E. Lee* in June and July of 1870.

The steamship also greatly stimulated all forms of local, national and international communications. Prior to the development of the telegraph in the 1830s, the letter was the primary means of communication over distances of more than a few miles. Since most communities in early nineteenth century Europe and America were located along waterways, the majority of the mails travelled aboard sailing vessels known as "packets," after their cargos of packets of letters. Led by the British, a number of governments recognized that the steamship could provide faster and more reliable transportation of the mails, and began in the 1840s to award substantial annual subsidies to those shipping companies willing to build and operate mail steamers. By 1857, steam packets had won the bulk of the mail trade from sailing vessels, and by 1880 had replaced them altogether.

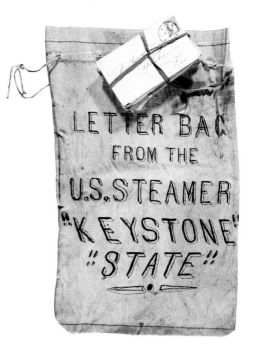

(*Left*) Packet of letters and mail bag from the steamer *Keystone State*, built in 1853. The ship belonged to Cornelius Vanderbilt's Atlantic and Pacific Mail Steamship Company prior to the Civil War (M-10113, Gift of Mrs. Bradford Wellman).

(*Right*) Selection of artifacts from Richard Byrd's second Antarctic campaign aboard the steamship *Bear*, from 1933–1935. Clockwise from upper left: *Bear* water keg, crampons, fragments of *Bear* figurehead and razor for Neptune ceremony (Respectively M-10794, M-14409, M-4396/14385, M-14358, Gifts of Henry C. Hallowell, William A. Robertson, and A. H. Waite).

Steamships were also primary factors in the development of another form of communications: the telegraph. Until 1858, use of this device was restricted to land-based applications, and only a few short underwater cables were in operation. In that year, however, under the direction of the engineer-businessman Cyrus W. Field, the two steamers *Agamemnon* and *Niagara* laid the first Transatlantic Telegraphic Cable. Without the superior maneuverability of the steamship, this delicate operation, which included the joining of the two halves of the cable in the mid-Atlantic, could not have been successfully completed, much less contemplated. This first transoceanic telegraph cable was followed within a few years by many others all over the world; today similar operations are carried out for telephone communications utilizing fiber-optical rather than electrical cables.

The steamship also played a central role in many of the most significant voyages of exploration in modern history. Among these are Robert Peary's North Pole expeditions aboard the specially designed steamer *Roosevelt* (1905–1909), Roald Amundsen's discovery of the Northwest Passage aboard the auxiliary fishing vessel *Gjøa* (1903–1905), and Rear Admiral Richard Byrd's Antarctic explorations, utilizing a variety of steam vessels (1928–1935). The superior speed, maneuverability and relative independence from weather conditions ideally suited these vessels for protracted exploration of the polar regions, where the ubiquitous icebergs and adverse climate made passages difficult even during the short summer months. These historic voyages of exploration added a considerable body of data, still being analyzed today, to man's scientific and humanistic knowledge of the extremes of our global environment.

The proliferation of steamship companies, both large and small, also played an important part in the history of emigration, immigration, and intercultural exchange in general. Despite the public and media emphasis on steamship tourism and the "First-Class Experience," it was the European emigrant travelling to America in the steerage class who provided a large portion of the revenues for steamship companies. During the years between 1815 and 1921, more than 30,000,000 people left their homelands (primarily in northern and western Europe) and settled in the United States. Aboard the sailing packets, these European emigrants were packed into noisy, unventilated and often unlighted densely packed double bunks. Little consideration was given to their dietary or sanitary requirements during the lengthy voyage. As a consequence, many immigrants arrived in the United States ill, exhausted and frightened, if they arrived at all. What scanty records exist for immigration to the United States in the first half of the nineteenth century indicate that the mortality rate over the course of a lengthy overseas voyage could reach as high as 10% among the very young and the very old. However, led by William Inman of the Liverpool-based Inman Line in the 1850s, the major steamship lines initiated a steerage class aboard their vessels, which provided far better living conditions and a much briefer passage. By the late nineteenth century, separate dining and sanitary facilities in steerage were standard, and lounges and semi-private cabins were available as well. In Europe, the emigrants were assisted by more than 18,000 agents for the steamship lines in arranging ticket purchases, transportation to the terminals, temporary lodging, and related services. At the other end of his journey the immigrant was met by American agents for the same lines, who helped them reach their final destinations. Smaller steamship trunk lines operating along the principal American waterways were

Chart of the Arctic in 1896, prior to the discovery of the North Pole by Robert Peary in 1909 (C-4679, Gift of the Essex Institute).

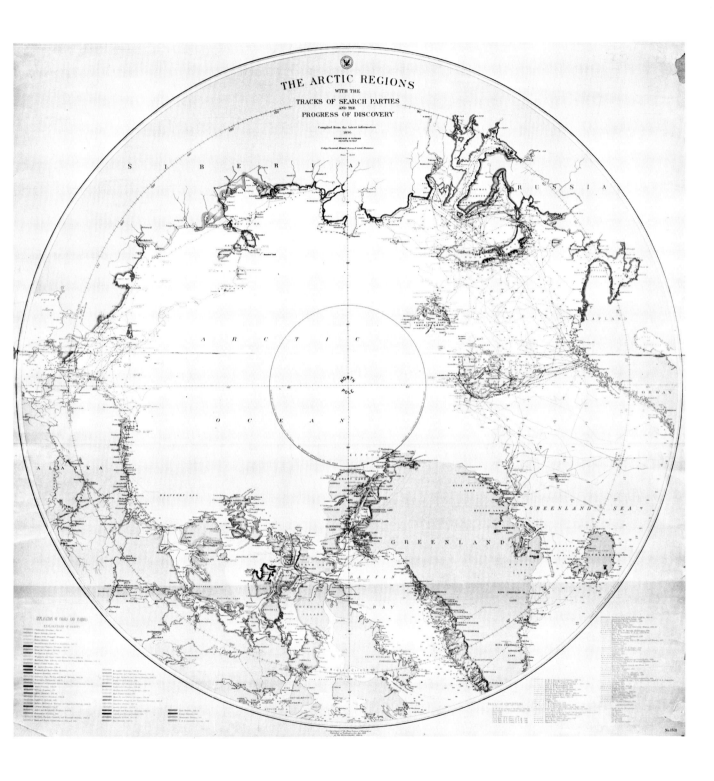

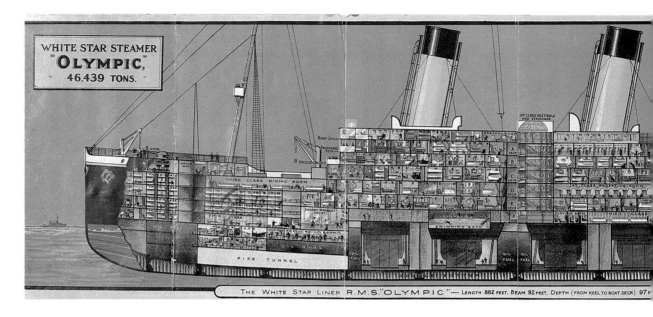

WHITE STAR STEAMER "OLYMPIC," 46,439 TONS.

THE WHITE STAR LINER R.M.S. "OLYMPIC" — LENGTH 882 FEET, BEAM 92 FEET, DEPTH (FROM KEEL TO BOAT DECK) 97 F

often the means chosen to disperse these enormous and diversified ethnic groups throughout North America, where they contributed to the burgeoning industrial and agricultural centers.

The steamship also played a pivotal role in the history of technology. Many of the major improvements in the steam engine and turbine during the nineteenth century and beyond occurred aboard ships, where the size, weight and fuel consumption of a power plant were critical factors. After 1840, when the transatlantic steamship traffic began, increased speed, power, safety and reliability also were added to the design parameters of the marine steam engine and propulsion systems. Intense competition among the steamship lines ensured rapid evolution, and the ensuing improvements were gradually incorporated back into the land-based industrial applications of the steam engine, such as mills, machine tool and die manufactories, mines, and other forms of transportation including the railroad locomotive and the steam-powered automobile. The refined principles of nineteenth century steam technology, as applied to the steamship, eventually resulted in the steam turbine, and thence to the modern oil-fired steam turbine in widespread use today on both land and sea.

(*Above*) Cross-section of the White Star liner *Olympic* of 1911 (M-13543, F. B. C. Bradlee Collection).

(*Right*) An 1851 print from the *Illustrated London News* depicting the squalid and overcrowded conditions in steerage aboard a transatlantic sailing packet (PMS Photo No. 18142).

(*Far right*) This small booklet dating to ca. 1880 describes the excellent conditions in the steerage class aboard the Inman Line's transatlantic steamer *City of Chester* (Phillips Library).

46,439. SPEED 22½ KNOTS. IN EQUIPMENT IT IS UNSURPASSED BY ANYTHING AFLOAT, AS CAN BE SEEN FROM THE DIAGRAMATIC PICTURE OF ITS INTERIOR.

EMIGRATION VESSEL.—BETWEEN DECKS.

IN THE

STEERAGE

OF THE

Inman Line

UNITED STATES AND ROYAL MAIL STEAMSHIP

City of Chester.

2 / PIONEERS OF MARINE STEAM TECHNOLOGY

The earliest known experimentation with steam engines was undertaken as early as the third century BC by the Greek mathematician and inventor Archimedes. A century or so later, the philosopher Hero of Alexandria designed a device that used steam power to open and close the doors of an Egyptian temple, although it is not recorded whether the device ever worked successfully or was even built. These engines were little more than "philosophical toys," however, and it was not until the eighteenth century that the steam engine saw practical development in western Europe. The earliest examples, as produced by Denis Papin (1647–1714) and Thomas Newcomen (1663–1729), were specifically designed to pump water either out of flooded mines or into the upper levels of tall commercial or residential buildings. Although sporadic attempts were made to put these crude and rather inefficient engines into watercraft, these efforts seldom yielded enough positive results to warrant further experimentation. The boats either blew up, sank, lacked sufficient power to breast a tide or current, or their builders lacked enough interest or capital for continued development. In the years around 1800 in Europe, there was very little incentive or encouragement for such ventures, for a variety of reasons. During this early experimental period, steam engines were very large and heavy, taking up a great deal of space that might otherwise be used for cargo or passengers. Moreover, the inland waterways in Europe were comparatively short, and the majority were paralleled by roads along which wagons and stagecoaches could travel faster than watercraft. Reliable sources of fuel were also a problem; most of Europe's best timber had long since been consumed by shipbuilding and other interests, and coal was not yet available in sufficient quantities to guarantee a steady supply. To these factors may be added the inherent conservatism of the shipbuilding industry, which throughout history had resisted rapid and radical change in favor of the more familiar and traditional ship designs and construction methods. By contrast, conditions were very different in America, and it was here that the earliest practical steamboats were produced.

Early advertising broadside from 1827 promoting steamboat travel on Long Island Sound (PMS Photo No. 6451).

In the United States, most of the inland and coastal waterways along which settlements were located were far longer than their European counterparts, and there were few decent roads connecting the communities. Consequently, a higher proportion of trade was waterborne than was the case in Europe. Timber for fuel was also readily available along the principal waterways, making it easy to set up local fuel depots. In addition, the savings in manpower promised by the steamboat inventors for their vessels was a real factor in early America, where the population base was still underdeveloped in relation to the growing requirements of industry and agriculture. Finally, the shipbuilding industry, still very new in America in the first half century of its independence, had fewer traditions and conventions than in Europe to hamper developments in new fields of technology.

Among the American steamboat pioneers, John Fitch (1743–1798) is traditionally accorded pride of precedence. Born on a small farm in Windsor, Connecticut, Fitch was removed from school at the age of eight to help his father with the crops. As a young man, he apprenticed himself to a number of craftsmen, including a clockmaker, a brass founder, and a silversmith,

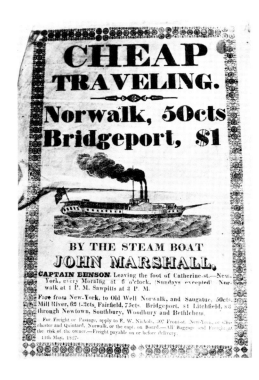

under whose collective tutelage he developed considerable mechanical abilities. A strong entrepreneurial spirit surfaced during the American Revolution, during which Fitch became a very successful gunsmith and merchant. With his profits from the war he secured warrants for extensive properties in the Northwest Territory along the Ohio River. While exploring these lands, Fitch also picked up the additional skills of surveying and mapping.

Fitch's initial few contacts with the sea were disastrous. At the age of seventeen, he ran away to sea but deserted before his ship even left port, on account of rough handling from the mate. Later, in March of 1782, while en route to see his newly-acquired lands in the Northwest Territory, his boat went aground on the Ohio River and he and his party were captured by Indians. Six months later, after a prisoner exchange with the British, he returned to New York from the Great Lakes via a ship down the St. Lawrence and along the New England coast. His personal account of the voyage confessed: "I much dreaded the going round by sea as I was born a natural coward to the water . . . . I had a great mind to desert, but could not get any to accompany me . . . ."

Nevertheless, during an idle period in 1785, Fitch conceived the idea of a boat for which an engine propelled by steam power rather than man or the wind would supply the motive force. Contemporary records seem to indicate that he arrived at the idea independently, unaware of similar experiments both in America and overseas. Utilizing his entrepreneurial and mechanical skills, in the latter portion of 1785 Fitch approached a number of influential individuals and organizations, including the Congress, several state legislatures, George Washington and Benjamin Franklin, seeking endorsements and financial backing. He managed to finance a small steamboat company in the amount of $300.00, by selling copies of the maps he had made during his western trips and on the strength of fourteen-year monopolies for steam navigation granted by the states of Delaware, New Jersey, New York and Pennsylvania. However, undercapitalization of his company, compounded by personal and political difficulties, delayed the formal test of his steamboat until the middle of 1787. Another source of delay was Fitch's refusal, for reasons of his own, to utilize existing steam engine technology already developed in England by James Watt; as a result he and his partner Henry Voight, a German watchmaker, were virtually forced to reinvent the atmospheric steam engine from scratch. In August of 1787 the two partners

Nineteenth century print of the early British steamboat by Millar, Taylor and Symington in the form of a catamaran, dating to 1788. Two paddlewheels were set between the twin hulls of the vessel, which was approximately 25 feet long (FLH Pr. 442, Francis Lee Higginson, Jr. Collection).

(*Right*) Advertising broadside circulated by John Fitch in 1785, indicating his intention to sell maps in order to finance his steamboat venture (PMS Photo No. 22714, Courtesy of the Library of Congress).

(*Middle right*) John Fitch's drawing of his adaptation of the Newcomen atmospheric engine, and his ratchet system for transferring the reciprocal engine motion to the paddles, ca. 1790 (PMS Photo No. 22717, Courtesy of the Library of Congress).

(*Far right*) Portrait of John Fitch from a contemporary illustration (PMS Photo No. 22722).

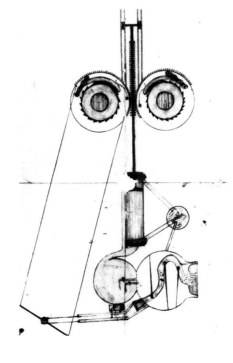

successfully tested their first steamboat, which was moved by duck-leg paddles, along the Delaware River outside Philadelphia, but the vessel proved to move too slowly and Fitch and Voight returned to the drawing board. However, the vessel had attracted favorable attention from several members of the Constitutional Convention then meeting in Philadelphia, and Fitch was able to secure another monopoly from the state of Virginia, despite the fact that this was the home state of his chief rival, James Rumsey (1743–1792). This monopoly marked the beginning of an abiding emnity between the two inventors that was to occupy a critical role in the future development of their respective steamboats. During the next two years, both Rumsey and Fitch devoted more energy to disputing each other's claims of invention than to their vessels, and little substantive progress was made by either. Fitch's backers refused further funding on account of a series of pamphlets published by Rumsey, and it was not until May of 1790 that he was able to test another steamboat on the Delaware. This vessel was far more satisfactory than the earlier one, and over the summer and fall of that year it operated with few breakdowns a total distance of 2000–3000 miles between Philadelphia and Trenton, with regular stops at Burlington, Bristol, and Bordentown. Although the vessel was faster (6–8 mph) and less expensive by half (5 shillings) than the stagecoach to Trenton, it was a commercial failure. Travellers seemed to prefer the latter, more familiar mode of transportation, and the little vessel was laid up in the fall of 1790, never to run again.

During that same year, at the urgings of another steamboat inventor, the wealthy and influential New Jersey politician Col. John Stevens (1749–1838), the Federal government instituted a patent commission, later known as the U.S. Patent Office, expressly to settle the claims of the numerous rival steamboat inventors. Although the makeup of the commission (the Attorney General and the Secretaries of War and State) indicated the importance attached by the federal government to the steamboat's potential, the scheduled hearings were delayed for over a year. Since the promise of an exclusive patent had been one of the chief attractions for the backers of both Fitch and Rumsey, these delays caused considerable hardships, and both men were forced to travel to Europe to raise additional funds. It was perhaps during this frustrating period that Fitch penned the following verses, preserved among the Peter Force Papers in the Library of Congress:

Preliminary sketch by John Fitch of one of his early steamboat designs, ca. 1785–1790 (PMS Photo No. 22715, Courtesy of the Library of Congress).

Opposing pamphlets written in 1788 by the rival steamboat inventors Rumsey and Fitch, each of whom was attempting to establish precedence for a patent application (PMS Photo No. 22712 (left), 22711 (right), Courtesy of the Library of Congress).

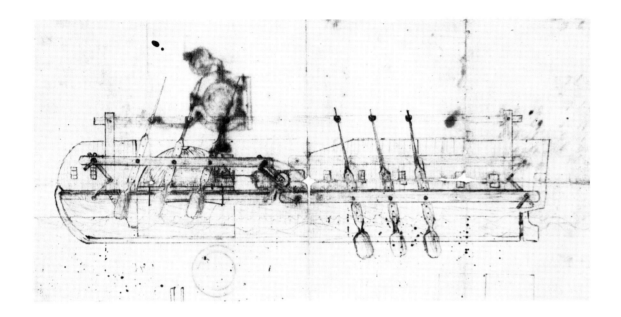

A

SHORT

TREATISE

ON THE APPLICATION OF

S T E A M,

WHEREBY IS CLEARLY SHEWN,

FROM

ACTUAL EXPERIMENTS,

THAT

S T E A M

MAY BE APPLIED TO PROPEL

BOATS OR *VESSELS*

OF ANY BURTHEN AGAINST RAPID CURRENTS WITH GREAT VELOCITY.

GREAT VELOCITY.

The same principles are also introduced with Effect, by a Machine of a simple and cheap Construction, for the purpose of raising Water sufficient for the working of

GRIST OR SAW MILLS.

AND *for* WATERING MEADOWS *and* OTHER AGRICULTURAL PURPOSES.

By JAMES RUMSEY,

OF BERKELEY COUNTY, *Virginia*.

PHILADELPHIA,

PRINTED BY JOSEPH JAMES: CHESNUT-STREET.

M,DCC,LXXXVIII.

THE

ORIGINAL

STEAM-BOAT

SUPPORTED;

OR,

A REPLY

TO

MR. JAMES RUMSEY's PAMPHLET.

SHEWING THE

TRUE PRIORITY

OF

JOHN FITCH,

AND THE

FALSE DATINGS, &c.

OF

JAMES RUMSEY.

PHILADELPHIA:

PRINTED BY ZACHARIAH POULSON, JUN. ON THE WEST SIDE OF FOURTH-STREET, BETWEEN MARKET AND ARCH-STREETS.

M DCC LXXXVIII.

Original boiler and engine from John Stevens' earliest steamboat, 1804 (PMS Photo No. 22723, Courtesy of the Smithsonian Institution).

Modern model of James Rumsey's second steamboat of 1787, which was propelled by a hydraulic jet (PMS Photo No. 22724, Courtesy of the Smithsonian Institution).

For full the scope of seven years
Steam Boats exited hopes & fears
In me, but now I see it plain
All furthe progress is in vain
And am resolved to quit a Scheming
And be nolonger of pattents dreaming
As for my partners *Dam them all*
They took me up to let me fall
For when my scheme was near perfection
It proved abortive by their defection
They let it stop for want of Rhines
Then swore the cause of failer mines.

These delays and problems proved terminal for both inventors. Rumsey died in 1792, and Fitch never built another steamboat. Instead, he returned in 1796 to his property in Kentucky, and sold three hundred acres of prime land to a local tavern owner in exchange for two pints of whiskey per day until he died, which he assured his supplier would not take long. He hastened the process by hoarding a supply of opium pills prescribed him for insomnia, and died of an overdose in 1798, a sad, defeated man whose abilities were unappreciated and achievements unrecognized in his own time.

The next American steamboat pioneer of note was the Pennsylvanian Robert Fulton (1765–1815), who is credited with having produced the first commercially successful steam-powered vessel. From a background remarkably similar to Fitch's, Fulton developed an early proficiency in jewelry making and miniature painting. This latter skill was especially important, for it provided him an introduction to the political, scientific and literary communities both in America and overseas. The patronage of these groups would later prove instrumental in his steamboat endeavors. While travelling in England in the 1790s, Fulton acquired a strong engineering and mechanical background through designing canal and mill machinery. Throughout his exceptionally prolific career, steamboats occupied only a minor portion of his considerable energies; he also developed submarines, torpedos, explosive mines, canal and mill machinery, a magic lantern, and other mechanical and manufacturing processes. Insofar as steamboats were concerned, Fulton was always more powerfully motivated by profit than by precedence. He had access to, and made free use of concepts already developed by his predecessors, notably Fitch, Rumsey and Robert R. Livingston in America and

Pair of early nineteenth century Gragg bentwood chairs originally belonging to Robert Fulton (M-14782/83, Gift of Mrs. John F. Fulton).

Robert Fulton's most famous steamboat, the *North River* of 1807, popularly known as the *Clermont*. Shown here in 1810 after being rebuilt (FLH Pr. 107, Francis Lee Higginson, Jr. Collection).

Desblancs, Jouffroy, Stanhope and Boulton and Watt in Europe. His first steamboat, built in France in 1802, was the result of thoroughly modern research methodology involving hull, engine and propulsion systems calculations and model testing prior to the construction of a full-scale ship. In collaboration with the American inventor Robert Livingston, Fulton rented a French 8-horsepower engine and designed a twelve foot diameter paddlewheel system, setting them both into a wooden hull 70 feet long. Before it could be tested, the boat sank during a storm; when refloated, its performance was disappointing and it was laid up.

After many years in England and France devoted to refining and promoting his submarine, Fulton returned to America and began developing his second and most famous steamboat, once again taking the wealthy and influential Livingston as his partner. Initially called simply *The Steamboat*, later *The North River Steamboat*, and ultimately registered as *The North River Steamboat of Clermont*, this vessel's name has been shortened by posterity to *Clermont*. Contemporary accounts of this vessel are scanty, and images are even rarer; however, a few details of her construction can be pieced

Engine and machinery from Fulton's *North River*, with modern paddles (PMS Photo No. 22725, Courtesy of the Smithsonian Institution).

Bronze medal issued by the American Numismatic Society in 1909 to commemorate the Hudson-Fulton Celebration. Beneath the portrait of Fulton are the allegorical figures of Commerce, Steam Navigation and History, from left to right (M-15523, Gift of M. David Schaeffer).

together. Somewhere between 133 and 150 feet in length, her decks were marked by masts at either end. The engine, which was imported from the British manufacturers Boulton and Watt, sat exposed in the middle of the vessel, surmounted by a high smokestack. The long, narrow flat-bottomed hull was propelled by large sidewheel paddles 15 feet in diameter; initially the paddles were uncovered, but later they were boxed in as the result of deliberate damage by sailing vessels. After her maiden voyage, a round trip up the Hudson River between New York and Albany in four days beginning 17 August 1807, the *North River* was strengthened and fitted out with bunks in her cabins and other amenities. Aside from a rebuilding the following winter, the *North River* operated at a modest profit for her owners until laid up in 1814. When fully booked, she carried around 90 passengers, including 54 in three cabins and the remainder on deck. Despite the relative success of the *North River*, it should be noted that both her top speed and the total distance travelled were less than the corresponding figures for Fitch's steamboat nearly two decades earlier.

Building upon his success with the *North River*, Fulton continued to build steamboats until his death in 1815, picking up several critical patents and monopolies along the way. Among his 21 steamboats are included such milestones as the first specially-designed ferry boats, the *New Orleans* of 1811 (the first steamer on the Mississippi), the *Demologos* of 1814 (the world's earliest naval steamboat), and the *Chancellor Livingston* of 1816,

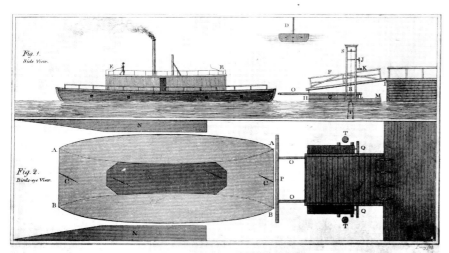

Fig. 1.
Side View.

Fig. 2.
Birds-eye View.

FULTON'S-STEAM FERRY BOAT.

Early nineteenth century print of one of the first steam-propelled ferry boats, designed by Robert Fulton ca. 1810 (M-11303, F. B. C. Bradlee Collection).

which was not completed until after his death. This large and luxurious passenger steamer, which cost $125,000 in contemporary currency, set a new standard for passenger accommodations, and incorporated all of the technical experience and expertise Fulton had acquired over a lengthy and most productive career. In general, Fulton's success, which was attributable to a combination of personal skills, timing, and the ability to synthesize others' achievements with his own, demonstrated to the world that the steamboat was a practical and viable alternative to the sailing vessel, and set the stage for rapid future developments in marine steam technology.

DEVELOPMENTS IN MARINE STEAM TECHNOLOGY

Broadly speaking, the technology of commercial sailing vessels had changed comparatively little during the seventeenth and eighteenth centuries. Around 1800, however, the addition to a ship's hull of a mechanical engine, its fuel supply, and the related machinery needed to transfer its reciprocating motion into motion in the water required extensive modifications in ship design. Just as sailing vessels gradually increased in size over time, so too did steamships, once their practicality was established. This in turn resulted in an increase over time in the size and complexity of the related power and propulsion systems required to move these large vessels safely and quickly through the water.

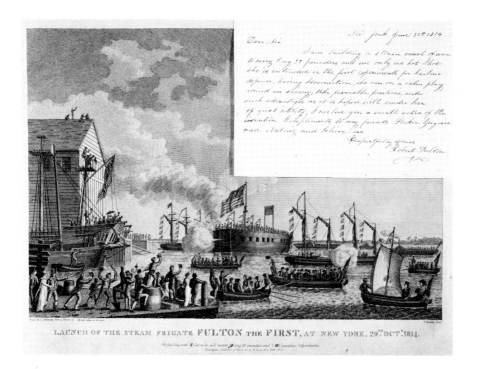

LAUNCH OF THE STEAM FRIGATE FULTON THE FIRST, AT NEW YORK, 29TH OCT.T 1814.

In 1814 Robert Fulton designed the first American steam-propelled naval vessel, *Fulton the First*, shown here with a letter he wrote concerning its armament and purpose (M-2851 [Print]; Phillips Library, War of 1812 Papers [Letter]).

The *Chancellor Livingston*, Fulton's finest steamship, was completed shortly after Fulton's death in 1815 and was used on Long Island Sound and along the Maine coast until 1834. The ladies' cabin was on the upper deck aft of the engine room, and the gentlemen's cabin was below and forward of the small deckhouses at the bow (M-11243, Gift of Mr. and Mrs. James A. Doughty).

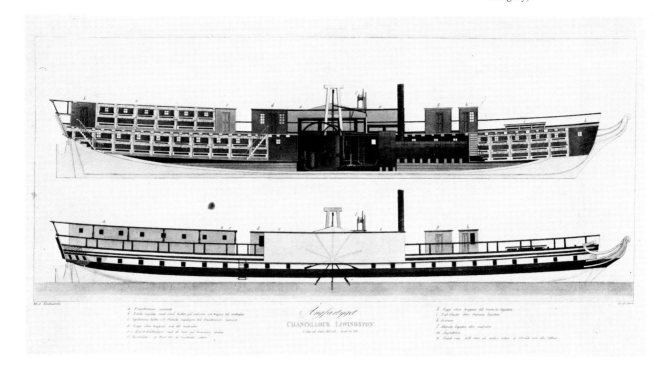

CHANCELLOUR LIVINGSTON

Power Plants

The earliest steam engines used aboard ships were relatively simple variations of the Newcomen or atmospheric engine, initially developed by the Englishman Thomas Newcomen around 1712. In its simplest form, this engine comprised a heavily weighted piston encased in a cylinder. Steam was fed into the cylinder below the piston head; as it condensed, it created a partial vacuum which helped push the piston downward, assisted by atmospheric pressure. The resulting reciprocal motion was transferred to horizontal or rotary motion by means of a large overhead beam attached to the piston head by a connecting rod, with a ratchet or circular gear at its opposite end. These engines were generally too heavy, bulky, and consumed too much fuel to be practical for marine applications however, and their use was restricted to the experimental years of the late eighteenth century. Fitch's drawings show that he was experimenting with a Newcomen-type engine, although more advanced engines were available to him in 1787. Working around the period of the American Revolution, the Scotsman James Watt (1736–1819), who invented the concept of "horsepower," improved on the

(*Left*) Schematic of a single-acting Newcomen or atmospheric engine, ca. 1705, illustrating how the steam was introduced below the piston head (PMS Photo No. 22721).

(*Right*) In James Watt's revolutionary double-acting steam engine, steam was alternately introduced above and below the piston head to force it to move up and down within its cylinder (PMS Photo No. 22729).

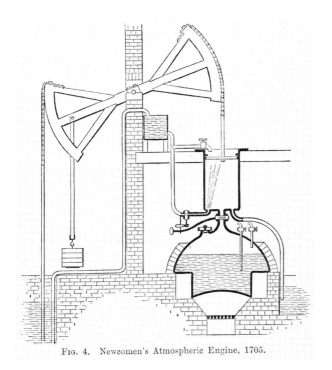

Fig. 4. Newcomen's Atmospheric Engine, 1705.

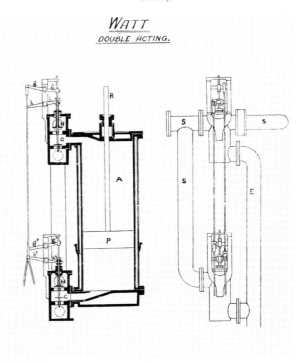

WATT
DOUBLE ACTING.

atmospheric engine by segregating the condensing chamber from the cylinder, and making the steam push the piston rather than atmospheric pressure. He also developed the double-acting engine, in which steam was used on both sides of the piston head to force it up and down, thereby doubling its efficiency. Watt's refinements, which also included the use of higher pressure steam than had previously been possible, formed the basis for all later steam engine technology on both land and sea. In 1788, Watt and his partner Boulton offered to enter into an exclusive agreement with James Rumsey to patent and distribute their engines in America. However, convinced by Benjamin Franklin and others of the superiority of his own ideas,

A sense of the immense size of one of the three triple-expansion engines of the *Kaiser Wilhelm der Grosse II* is provided by the two men in this illustration, one at lower left and one in the center (PMS Photo No. 19488).

Rumsey foolishly declined the terms offered, preferring instead to continue developing his own jet-boat principles. Later, in 1807, Robert Fulton purchased the third Boulton and Watt engine ever exported from England, to power his famous and successful *North River* steamboat.

One of the earliest types of engines to find widespread application aboard steamboats was the side lever engine, developed in England around 1810. Utilizing the basic principles of the simple steam engine, the primary innovation of the side lever involved the transmission of power from the cylinder to the crankshaft via a lever alongside the engine, rather than overhead. This arrangement permitted the power plant to be placed lower in the ship's hull, providing both a lower center of gravity and more space. The side lever engine was popular until around 1850, when it was replaced by the oscillating engine. This variation entailed cylinders which rocked on their axes on trunions, and allowed the pistons to be directly connected to the overhead crankshaft, thereby eliminating connecting rods. The overhead crankshaft transmitted the reciprocating engine motion into rotary motion, which turned a pair of paddlewheels. This engine type permitted fewer moving parts and a considerable savings in weight and space, which were the primary disadvantages of the earlier side lever engine.

The next major innovation in marine steam engine technology was the introduction of the compound engine in the 1850s. In this system, high pressure steam first entered a small, high pressure cylinder. Then, rather than being exhausted into a condenser or the air, the steam was recycled directly into a larger, low pressure cylinder before being vented off, so that the steam was used twice. The inverted compound engine, in which the steam cylinders were placed above rather than below the crankshaft, found great popularity aboard steamships that used propellers, since the propellers exited the ship's hull well below the waterline. The compound engine was used until the 1870s, when the triple-expansion engine was introduced. This engine type, and the quadruple-expansion engine which evolved from it around 1900, were simply natural extensions of the compound engine. Progressively lower pressure steam passed from the high pressure cylinder directly into two or three additional lower pressure cylinders respectively, before being vented off for condensing and recycling. In this way, more of the energy of the steam, which entered the high pressure cylinder of a

Turbine blade, 12″ long by 1″ wide, from the Cunard Liner *Mauretania*, which was dismantled in 1935 (M-9317, Francis Lee Higginson, Jr. Collection).

triple-expansion engine at a typical pressure of 150–190 pounds per square inch, could be harnessed than had been possible with the earlier types of engines.

The last major development in marine steam technology was the introduction in the 1890s of the steam turbine by the British engineer Charles Parsons. In the turbine, high pressure steam is introduced into a horizontal cylinder or casing, and sets into motion angled blades fixed axially onto a longitudinal rotor. The rotary motion of this drum is then transferred to the propeller shaft either directly or through a reduction gearing, providing a much simpler, smaller and more efficient source of power than the reciprocating engine. The first marine turbine was installed by Parsons in 1897 aboard the yacht *Turbinia*; its astonishing speed of 30 knots so impressed the onlookers that within only a few years of its introduction the turbine was adopted by the major naval and commercial fleets of the world.

The marine turbine remained popular through the first quarter of the twentieth century, after which it was gradually replaced by the diesel engine, developed around 1910. For almost all smaller naval and commercial engine-powered ships of the present day for which speed is not a major consideration, the marine diesel has been found to be the most efficient and reliable power plant.

Propulsion systems

After the engine, the next most critical element that had to be developed was the propulsion system, which drove the steamship through the water. Prior to the emergence of the paddlewheel, a number of different approaches to the problem of propulsion were taken by the early inventors, with varying degrees of success. Among these were John Fitch's "duck-leg" paddles, similar to oars, which were attached to a framework either along the side or off the stern of his vessels. Fitch also experimented, at least on the drawing board, with Archimedean screws and jet propulsion systems, and made a boat model with an "endless chain of paddles" along one side which he presented in 1785 to the American Philosophical Society in Philadelphia in support of his ideas. By contrast, James Rumsey, after testing a manually operated mechanical pole boat, elected to develop a jet propulsion system for his steamboat, following the advice of his patron Benjamin Franklin. While both Fitch's and Rumsey's systems did achieve limited success, neither was efficient enough to warrant further development by other inventors. Instead, most of the early pioneers turned to the paddlewheel for propelling their craft. This device was certainly not new; paddlewheels fitted to a capstan arrangement powered either by men or animals were used on smallcraft in ancient Egypt, and later appeared in China and the Mediterranean during the Middle Ages. In the early days of the steamboat, inventors installed the paddlewheels at a number of different locations along or abaft the hull before settling on the side of the vessel as the most efficient and practical spot for ocean-going vessels. Despite several disadvantages, the sidewheel paddle saw almost universal use aboard steamships until well past the middle of the nineteenth century, and sternwheel paddle steamers lasted even longer on inland waters, where shallow waters and narrow channels often prevented the sidewheel paddle or propeller from operating. Around 1840 a refinement was added to the paddle wheel in the form of a mechanical feathering device which ensured that the surface of each paddle was perpendicular to the water throughout its stroke.

One of the chief disadvantages of the sidewheel paddle was its tendency to lift out of the water on one side in a high sea, which could strain the engine and drivetrain. In addition, the efficiency of the paddlewheel was a factor of the draft of a vessel; if it were travelling light the floats barely reached

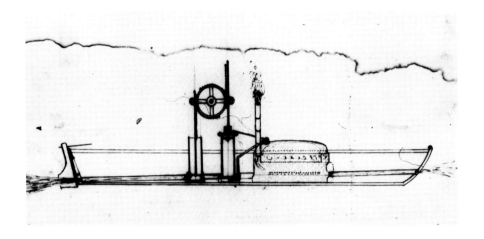

(*Top*) Fitch investigated a jet propulsion system for his steamboat before returning to a more orthodox concept, ca. 1785–1790 (PMS Photo No. 22716, Courtesy of the Library of Congress).

(*Bottom left*) Drawing by John Fitch of a "duck-leg" paddle system similar to the design he installed on his first steamboat, ca. 1785–1790 (PMS Photo No. 22710, Courtesy of the Library of Congress).

(*Bottom right*) John Fitch drawing of a helical screw propulsion system, ca. 1785–1790 (PMS Photo No. 22714, Courtesy of the Library of Congress).

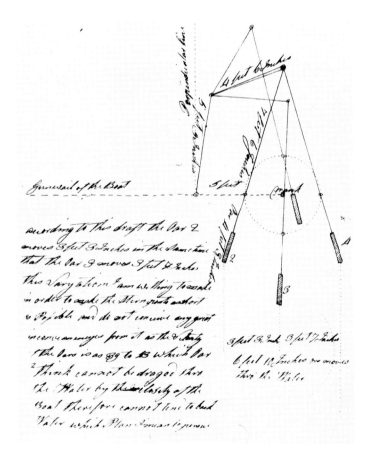

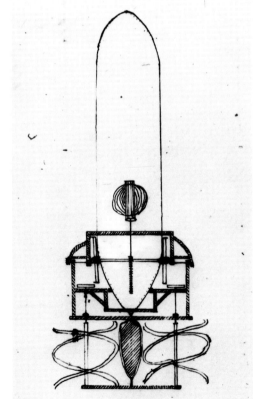

into the water, and if the ship was heavily laden, the floats could be too deeply immersed to perform properly. The paddlewheels and their boxes were also vulnerable to damage from striking floating objects. As a result, an alternate form of propulsion was sought by both naval and commercial shipping concerns.

Experimentation in Europe in the 1830s indicated that the propeller, a modern variant of the Archimedean screw, held the most promise. Although it was totally submerged beneath the hull of a vessel and was therefore more difficult to service than the paddlewheel, it was also far simpler with fewer moving parts, and needed servicing less often. Since it was underwater, it was also less likely to strike floating objects or be damaged by collision than the more prominent paddlewheel. In 1838, the British inventor who first patented the propeller, Francis Pettit Smith (1808–1874), sold

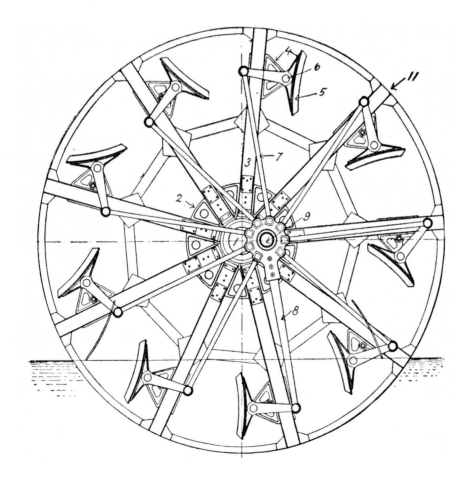

This illustration from the 1918 edition of *Audel's New Marine Engineers' Guide* illustrates the self-feathering sidewheel paddle, which ensured that the paddle float was always perpendicular to the water (PMS Photo No. 22731).

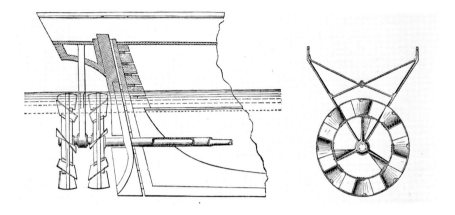

(*Left*) Propeller design ca. 1835 by John Ericsson, who is best remembered for his Civil War ironclad *Monitor.* Illustration from *A Treatise on the Screw Propeller*, 1855 (PMS Photo No. 22732).

(*Below*) The *Archimedes* of 1838 was one of the first successful propeller-driven commercial steamships. She was named after her helical propeller, which was an adaptation of the Archimedean screw (FLH Pr. 210, Francis Lee Higginson, Jr. Collection).

Eye-level photograph of the twin screws of the Cunard liner *Campania*, built in 1892. The massive bronze propellers turned at a speed of 84 revolutions per minute (PMS Photo No. 22733).

S.S. CAMPANIA. [CUNARD]

his patents to the Ship Propeller Company, which built the first large pro-peller-driven vessel, *Archimedes*, that same year. The helical propeller drove the *Archimedes* at a speed of nine knots, and its reliablity was proven during a circumnavigation of Great Britain in 1840. The propeller subsequently re-ceived the endorsement of the conservative British Admiralty in 1845, dur-ing trials of two identically built and powered frigates, the *Rattler* and the *Alecto*. The propeller-driven *Rattler* easily beat the paddle steamer *Alecto* in a hundred-mile race and in a tug-of-war, proving that the propeller was su-perior to the paddlewheel both in speed and power. Although the world's navies adopted it shortly thereafter, commercial steamship companies were somewhat slower to endorse its use for reasons both of conservatism and ex-cessive vibration, which made passengers nervous and uncomfortable. The Cunard Line did not build its last paddlewheeler until 1861, and its compet-itors finally phased out their paddle steamers a little later. Thereafter, right up to the present day, the propeller has been used almost without exception in all forms of engine-powered vessels.

3/COASTAL STEAMBOATS

New England and the East Coast

It was nearly a decade after the maiden voyage of Fulton's *North River* in 1807 that steamboats began operating in the northeastern United States. Among the reasons for the delay were the highly restrictive steamboat patents Fulton had taken out, which prevented other entrepreneurs from entering the field. By 1816, however, there were two steamboats on Long Island Sound, and one in Massachusetts. The latter vessel was built in Lowell in 1816 as a form of sidewheeler, with two wheels on each side connected by an endless chain with paddles or buckets spaced along its length. Little is known of this vessel aside from the fact that it carried passengers on the Merrimack River for at least the summer of 1816, and possibly longer. Considerably more information is preserved for the next steamboat in the state and the first in the Boston area, the *Massachusetts*, owned and operated by the Massachusetts Steam Navigation Company. This company, which was incorporated 16 June 1817 and capitalized in the amount of $330,000, commissioned the Philadelphia shipbuilder William M. Dodge and Company to build a steamboat to run between Boston and Salem, Massachusetts. From the beginning of its maiden voyage in April 1817 from Philadelphia to Salem, the *Massachusetts* encountered severe problems. Hit by a gale en route to Salem, the vessel's engine and paddles were damaged, and the ship took three weeks just to reach New York, under ignominious tow by two schooners. When it finally reached Salem in early June, crowds had to be fenced off so that three weeks' worth of additional repairs could be carried out. Although the damaged vessel generated much curiosity and speculation, it did not inspire much confidence in its ability to provide regular and reliable service to Boston. The diary of the Reverend William Bentley of Salem records prevailing local opinion of the steamboat in the entry for 3 July 1817:

> "The Steamboat returned [from her first trip to Boston] . . . . Another steam boat has burst the boiler bet. Newport and New London . . . . Ours has been under frequent

Coastal Steamboats

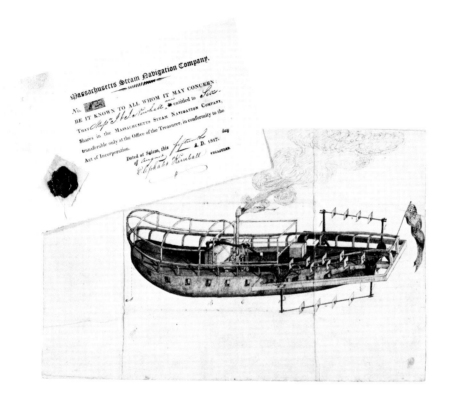

Massachusetts Steam Navigation Company stock certificate and drawing of the steamboat *Massachusetts* by its builder, William Dodge, dating to 1817 (Private Collection).

Engraved steel ticket plate and ticket for the 1817 steamboat *Massachusetts* (Left: M-13934, Right: M-8913, F. B. C. Bradlee Collection).

repairs, but rather less swift in its movements than was expected. It was said she would not return to Salem from the strength of prejudice against it . . . ."

During the summer of 1817 the *Massachusetts* operated at a loss between Salem and Hingham, Nahant, Marblehead, Gloucester and Portsmouth. Consequently the vessel was sold for $5,200 in November of 1817, and then sold again ten days later for the same sum. The Massachusetts Steam Navigation Company sued the builder Dodge for $20,000, the original cost of the vessel, blaming him for bad materials and shoddy workmanship. After a brief sojourn in debtor's prison, Dodge and a group of partners managed to settle with the original owners. Meanwhile, however, the *Massachusetts* had been wrecked off the coast of New Jersey while en route to North Carolina and Alabama for her new owners; bits and pieces of her were salvaged and may have been re-used in the construction of a later vessel of the same name.

Despite the New England steamboat's rather inauspicious beginning, including the wreck of the *Massachusetts* and the violent explosion of the wooden boiler aboard the *John Hancock* referred to in Bentley's diary entry steamboats were operating in the waters of every state in the Northeast by the middle 1820s. However, accidents such as boiler explosions, collisions, and groundings continued to occur with alarming frequency, and Congress was forced to enact legislation requiring periodic boiler inspections, the licensing of steamboat captains, pilots and engineers, running lights for night service, lifeboats and other lifesaving equipment. This cut drastically the number of accidents and steamboat traffic accordingly increased, with Boston, Providence, and New York serving as the primary hubs of activity. Regular steamboat lines with anywhere between one and fifteen vessels date from as far back as 1822 with the Livingston and Fulton Steam Navigation Company, which charged $10.00 for a one-way ticket between New York and Providence, with a stopover at Newport. Other lines starting in the 1830s, such as the Maine-based Sanford Line and the Boston and Bangor Line, extended service beyond the hub cities and their immediate neighbors to the smaller communities along the coast from Maine to New York and beyond. During the first half of the nineteenth century the majority of these lines operated as trunk services, providing local transportation of goods and passengers between cities and towns. Somewhat later, so-called "outside

Eastern Steamship Lines, Inc.

Steamer *City of Rockland*

Stations of Fire and Life Boat Crews

Port Life Boat Crews

BOAT No. 2 — Chief Officer in charge
Life boat men
Crew numbers " 2 - 4 - 6
" " 30 - 31

BOAT No. 4 — 1st Off. in charge
Life boat men " 13 - 4
Crew numbers " 13
" " 34 - 35 - 59

BOAT No. 4 A — Chief Engineer in charge
Life boat men Oiler " 1
Crew numbers Watertender " 1
Fireman " 17 - 18 - 19

BOAT No. 6 — 2nd Asst. Eng. in charge
Life boat men O.S. " 3
Crew numbers Watertender " 3
Fireman " 23 - 24 - 25

BOAT No. 6 A — Quartermaster " 1 in charge
Life boat men Freight Clerk
Crew numbers " 40 - 41 - 64

BOAT No. 8 — 3 Asst. Eng. in charge
Life boat men Watchman " 1
Crew numbers " 8 - 10 - 12
" " 44 - 45 - 65

BOAT No. 14 — in charge
Life boat men
Crew numbers

BOAT No. 16 — in charge
Life boat men
Crew numbers

Starboard Life Boat Crews

BOAT No. 1 — Captain in charge
Life boat men " 13 - 1
Crew numbers " 1 - 3 - 5
" " 28 - 29

BOAT No. 3 — 2nd Pilot in charge
Life boat men Watchman " 4
Crew numbers " 14 - 16
" " 32 - 33 - 56

BOAT No. 5 — 3rd Officer in charge
Life boat men 2. Watchman
Crew numbers " 15
" " 36 - 37 - 60 - 61

BOAT No. 5 — 1st Asst. Eng. in charge
Life boat men Oiler " 2
Crew numbers Watertender " 2
Fireman " 20 - 21 - 22

BOAT No. 5 A — Boatswain in charge
Life boat men Watchman " 2
Crew numbers Steward " 1
" " 38 - 39
" " 62 - 63

BOAT No. 7 — Watchman " 3 in charge
Life boat men " 13 - 3
Crew numbers " 7 - 9 - 11
" " 48 - 49 - 66

BOAT No. 13 — in charge
Life boat men
Crew numbers

BOAT No. 15 — in charge
Life boat men
Crew numbers

Port Life Raft Crews

RAFT No. 2 — Chief Steward in charge
Life boat men Chief Cook
Crew numbers Steward " 2
" " " 52

RAFT No. 4 — Watchman " 5 in charge
Life boat men 2nd Cook
Crew numbers " 50

RAFT No. 6 — Purser in charge
Life boat men " 47
Crew numbers " 51 - 53

RAFT No. 8 — in charge
Life boat men
Crew numbers

RAFT No. 10 — in charge
Life boat men
Crew numbers

RAFT No. 12 — in charge
Life boat men
Crew numbers

RAFT No. 14 — in charge
Life boat men
Crew numbers

RAFT No. 16 — in charge
Life boat men
Crew numbers

Starboard Life Raft Crews

RAFT No. 1 — Quartermaster " 2 in charge
Life boat men Cashier
Crew numbers " 42 - 43 - 58

RAFT No. 3 — 2nd Steward in charge
Life boat men Head Saloonman
Crew numbers " 46

RAFT No. 5 — Watchman " 6 in charge
Life boat men Radio Operator
Crew numbers " 54 - 55

RAFT No. 7 — in charge
Life boat men
Crew numbers

RAFT No. 9 — in charge
Life boat men
Crew numbers

RAFT No. 11 — in charge
Life boat men
Crew numbers

RAFT No. 13 — in charge
Life boat men
Crew numbers

RAFT No. 15 — in charge
Life boat men
Crew numbers

Port Fire Stations

FORWARD PUMP — 2nd Steward Watchman " 1
Crew numbers " 1 - 3 - 7 - 16 " 55

AFT PUMP — Watchman " 2
Crew numbers " 2 - 4 - 9 - Fireman " 27

HYDRANT No. 2 — Boatswain
Crew numbers " 13 - 3 " 23

HYDRANT No. 4 — Head Saloonman
Crew numbers 28 - 29 - 62

HYDRANT No. 6
Crew numbers 32 - 33 - 64

HYDRANT No. 8 — Watchman
Crew numbers " 11 - 13

HYDRANT No. 10
Crew numbers 38 - 39 - 57

HYDRANT No. 12
Crew numbers 42 - 43 - 59

HYDRANT No. 14 — 3rd Officer
Life boat men " 12 - 14

HYDRANT No. 16 — Oiler " 1

Starboard Fire Stations

FORWARD HAND PUMP
Crew numbers

AFT HAND PUMP
Crew numbers

HYDRANT No. 1 — Watchman " 3
Crew numbers " O.S. " 21 - 22

HYDRANT No. 3 — Boatswain
Crew numbers " 13 - 4

HYDRANT No. 5
Crew numbers 30 - 31 - 63

HYDRANT No. 7
Crew numbers 34 - 35 - 65 - 66

HYDRANT No. 9
Crew numbers " 36 - 37 - 56

HYDRANT No. 11
Crew numbers " 40 - 41 - 58

HYDRANT No. 13 — Watchman " 5
Crew numbers " 51 - 13

HYDRANT No. 15 — Chief Cook 2nd Cook Watchman

Important Notice

MUSTER OF CREW

Captain in general charge, other officers or able seamen in charge of their respective boats or rafts after reporting to their proper stations shall await orders from the captain before clearing away.

At the sound of the boat alarm every member of the ship's crew not in charge of boats shall report to their proper boat or raft stations and await orders from the officer or able seaman in charge of their respective boats.

A licensed officer or able seaman in charge of his boat or raft shall have a list of her life boat men and other members of his crew and he shall see that the men placed under his orders are acquainted with their several duties such as making fast or clearing away, boat falls, shipping, rudder, screwing down automatic plug cap, rowing and handling of oars, etc.

It shall be the duty of the steward to instruct certain men of his department as to their duties in relation to the passengers at a time of emergency.

These duties shall include:
(a) Warning passengers.
(b) See that they are dressed and have put on their life belts in the proper manner.
(c) Assembling passengers.
(d) Keeping order in the passage ways and on stairways and generally controlling the movements of passengers.

Fire extinguishers and chemical engine shall be used in a time of emergency and at the sound of the emergency bell in the crew's quarters members of the crew assigned to the chemical engine or fire extinguishers shall report to their proper stations registered on fire annunciator as per station bill prescribed for this purpose.

Oiler No. 1 in charge of water tight door at tunnel

Safety regulations for the Eastern Steamship Co.'s steamer *City of Rockland*, built in 1901 (M-6935, F. B. C. Bradlee Collection).

Passes such as this example from Sanford's Independent Line dating to 1875 were commonly issued to officers of major railroads as a courtesy (Phillips Library, F. B. C. Bradlee Collection).

Travellers' map issued by the Joy Line in 1905, illustrating its outside line between Boston and New York prior to the opening of the Cape Cod Canal (Phillips Library, McRoberts Collection).

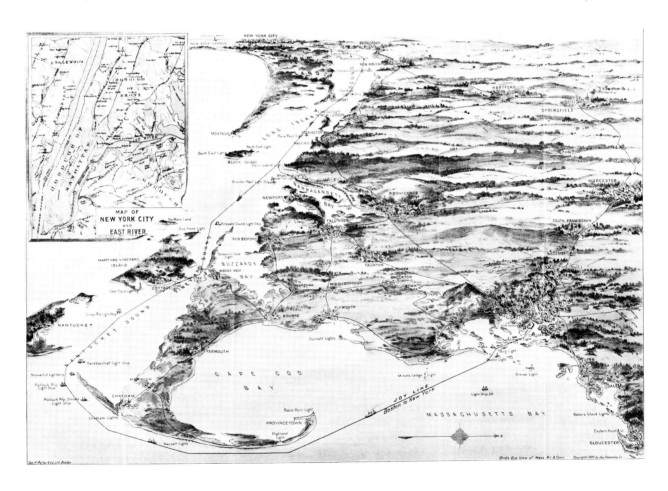

lines" were added which provided direct connections between the major cities with few if any local stops. Due to weather conditions, operations were primarily seasonal, ending in November and beginning again in the early spring. Of all of the northeastern steamship lines operating before 1900, only the Old Fall River Line, inaugurated in 1847, provided year-round service. Most of the lines offered both passenger and freight service, although space for freight, which consisted primarily of New England textiles, seafood and leather products bound for the New York market, was limited on account of the large amounts of fuel (first wood, later coal) that had to be carried on board. The earliest steamer of the Boston and Bangor Line, the *Bangor* of 1833 (160 feet, 400 tons), required 25 cords of hardwood for a single one-way voyage between Bangor and Boston. Pound for pound, passengers were a far more profitable cargo than freight.

A typical New England steamer of the mid-nineteenth century measured around 200 feet in length and 25–30 feet in beam over the guards. Power was normally supplied by a walking beam engine set amidships, propelling sidewheel paddles. The boilers were often set outside the ship proper over the paddle guards, rather than deep inside the hull, as a safety measure. Sails were commonly carried on these vessels, both as a source of auxiliary power and as a backup should there be engine problems. Wooden hulls were the rule even on the largest steamers until around 1890, when metal hulls (iron and steel) came into widespread use both on steamships and on larger sailing vessels as well. Prior to the changeover to steel, one of the most characteristic features of the New England wooden steamship was an external "hogging frame" or truss, visible on the upper deck, which helped to provide longitudinal strength and prevent the wooden hull from sagging as a result of the weight of the engine and constant pounding through rough waters. A majority of the larger steamboats operating in New England and the Northeast were built in New York and Pennsylvania, with smaller numbers constructed in Delaware, Maine, New Jersey and Rhode Island.

Passenger accommodations aboard these steamships varied from merely comfortable to outrageously luxurious and extravagant. The early boats had separate cabins in the hold for ladies and gentlemen. Meals were initially included in the ticket price, and were served in the after ladies' cabin, which generally had a higher quality of furnishings. The gentlemen's cabin, or saloon, was normally in the forward hold; both sets of cabins had free berths

The *Bangor*, built in 1833, was the first steamship belonging to the Boston and Bangor Steamship Company, and operated between Boston and Bangor until 1841. The following year she was sold to the Turkish government, and at one point in her career carried Muslim pilgrims to Egypt en route to Mecca (M-11363, F. B. C. Bradlee Collection).

Oil by James Bard of the Sanford steamer *Ocean* of 1849, which operated between Boston and Bath. The *Ocean*, considered one of the finest steamboats of her day, sank in Boston Harbor in 1854 after a collision with the Cunard liner *Canada* (M-4265, F. B. C. Bradlee Collection).

along their perimeters which passengers could use during overnight trips. Around 1850 private staterooms were added to the larger boats, and a surcharge was added for meals. As the boats gradually increased in size, additional decks, rooms and lounges were added for specialized activities such as eating, socializing, drinking and smoking. Particular attention was paid by the steamship owners to the more public and therefore the more visible dining rooms and grand saloons, where the decoration and furniture were as lavish as possible in order to lure passengers away from competitors' vessels.

After the end of the Civil War, there was a tremendous increase in tourism, and the steamship lines responded by adding to their regular routes excursion trips to such popular vacation spots as Bar Harbor, Nahant, Nantasket Beach, Cape Cod and various islands off the coast of Maine, Massachusetts and on Long Island Sound. Somewhat later, in 1888, one line even advertised one of the earliest winter cruises ever offered to the

Steamship poster of the Providence and Stonington Steamship Company's *Connecticut* of 1889, illustrating her luxurious interior (M-7248, F. B. C. Bradlee Collection).

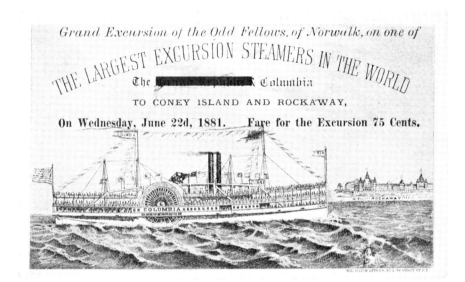

Sailing card from 1881 advertising an excursion aboard the side-wheeler *Columbia* to Coney Island and Rockaway Beach (Phillips Library).

Typical sightseeing brochures of the Fall River Line dating to 1886 (left) and 1888 (right), outlining sailing schedules, fares, itineraries, and the like (Phillips Library, McRoberts Collection).

public: a 60-day excursion for 25 people from Boston to the West Indies. By this time, competition for the tourist trade was so strong among steamship lines that to generate additional trade such amenities as electric lights and running water were commonly added aboard steamships long before they found widespread use on land.

One of the best known and longest-lived steamship lines in the Northeast was the Old Fall River Line, which began operations as the Bay State Steamboat Company in 1847. Initially this line operated a daily service of two boats between Boston and New York, with rail service from Boston to Fall River and the remainder by boat. In this way, the long water route around Cape Cod could be avoided. In 1869 the line was merged with several others by the colorful "Admiral" Jim Fisk, who adopted his title in ironic emulation of "Commodore" Cornelius Vanderbilt. Fisk attracted much new business for his various steamship lines, joined together under the name of the Narragansett Steamship Company, by adding to his vessels such novelties as staff bands and hundreds of canaries in golden cages, and by parading among the saloon passengers decked out in a gaudy admiral's uniform. In 1872 Fisk died, and the Fall River Line was reorganized into the Old Colony Steamboat Company, itself a branch of the Old Colony Railroad. This marked the beginning of the line's control by the growing railroad system in the Northeast, which lasted until its demise. Ten years later, in 1882, the Fall River Line began building a series of famous Long Island Sound steamers, known for their ever-increasing size and luxury. The foremost of these famous "Queens of the Sound" was the *Pilgrim* of 1882, which counted among its firsts the earliest double hull (of iron) in the United States, and the earliest fire-proofing, automatic fire alarms and electric lighting (installed by Thomas Alva Edison) embodied in the design. The *Pilgrim* also had one of the largest walking beam engines ever produced for a ship, and consumed an average of 85 tons of coal per voyage. She had overnight accommodations for 1,200 passengers, whose every want was fulfilled by "interior arrangements and furnishings . . . . equal to anything found in the fitting of the most elegant caravansary on land," according to one writer. The *Pilgrim* was among the most popular vessels on Long Island Sound until 1894, when the Fall River Line put into service the largest sidewheel paddle steamer ever built at the time: the *Priscilla*, which measured 440½

The *Eudora*, built in 1843, was the first steamer of the Fall River Line, and one of the first propellers on Long Island Sound. She was sent out to California during the Gold Rush of 1849, after which she dropped out of the records (M-11376, F. B. C. Bradlee Collection).

Steamship poster of the Old Fall River liner *Pilgrim* of 1882 framed by the Brooklyn Bridge, itself completed in 1883. *Pilgrim* served her owners faithfully until scrapped in New London in 1915 (M-5919).

feet long by 93 feet over the guards, and could accommodate 1,500 over-night guests. Her grand saloon alone measured 143 feet long by 30 feet wide. In a paroxysm of hyperbole, one copywriter speculated that had Robert Fulton seen the *Priscilla*, ". . . he might have taken leave of his senses, through fear that some terrible delusion or mental malady had seized upon him, a sort of retributive visitation consequent upon his temerity in rivalling the forces of nature."

The last passenger vessel the Old Fall River Line built was also the greatest in every sense of the word. The *Commonwealth* of 1908, with four full decks, was the largest sidewheel paddle steamer ever built for salt water service in America, measuring 437.9 feet long by 95 feet over the guards, and 5980 tons gross. Her compound engine developed 11,000 horsepower and drove her through the water at a speed of 23 miles per hour. Rumored to have cost $2,000,000, the *Commonwealth* incorporated no fewer than seven distinct architectural styles in her interior decoration, which was provided by the prestigious New York firm of Pottier and Stymus. These included Venetian Gothic (main saloon), Louis XVI (corridors), Empire, Adams, Louis XV (special rooms), late sixteenth century Italian/Spanish (cafe) and "Modern English" (quarter deck). The *Commonwealth* even had a special bridal suite to accommodate honeymooners.

These well-known steamers, and other less-known vessels of the Fall River Line and its competitors continued to operate profitably in the Northeast until the United States entered World War I, when service was drastically cut and many vessels were requisitioned for the war effort. In 1916, the Cape Cod Canal was opened, which further cut into the revenues of those steamship lines dependent upon railway connections for part of their service. In fact, this was nearly all of the steamship lines in the Northeast; with the exception of the Eastern Steamship Company and the Colonial Line, virtually all of the remainder by 1910 were wholly or in part owned by the New York, New Haven and Hartford Railroad—19 lines in all. A further factor in the decline of service was the closing of the Naval Training Station in Newport, Rhode Island at the end of World War I, which cut deeply into freight and passenger business. An even stronger blow was the stock market crash of 1929 and the resulting Depression; in 1935 the parent railroad went bankrupt, and in a reorganization in 1937 closed down its few remaining steamship services, including the Fall River Line. During its

Steamship poster with illustration by Fred Pansing of the Old Fall River liner *Priscilla* of 1894, against the New York skyline. *Priscilla* served the line for 43 years before being scrapped (M-11350, F. B. C. Bradlee Collection).

Oil painting by Antonio Jacobsen of the last Fall River liner, the *Commonwealth* of 1908 (M-5117, F. B. C. Bradlee Collection).

Fall River Line
OLD COLONY STEAMBOAT COMPANY
NEW YORK   BOSTON

Photograph of grand saloon of the *Commonwealth*, piled high with laundry from the staterooms (PMS Photo No. 22742).

(*Top left*) Mahogany sign from the *Commonwealth* (M-19328, Gift of James Pettee).

(*Top right*) Selection of tableware from the New England Steamship Company, which was owned by the New York, New Haven and Hartford Railroad (From upper left, M-18723, M-18722, M-18721, M-18724, M-18717, M-18720, Gift of J. Welles Henderson).

(*Bottom*) Eastern Steamship Lines advertising sign from 1924. Eastern was the Fall River Line's strongest competitor, and its two sisterships *Boston* and *New York* boasted hot and cold running water in the staterooms, among other alluring features (M-6995, F. B. C. Bradlee Collection).

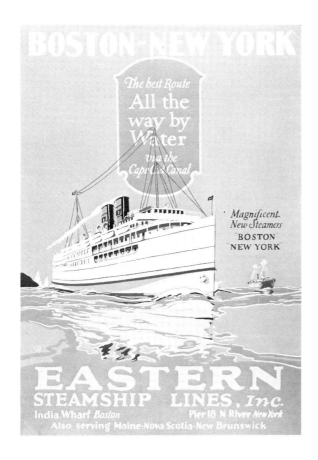

ninety-one years of service, the famous company had compiled a remarkable record for safety and reliability unequalled by any other form of transportation known to man: not a single ship lost by collision and only one passenger death among the more than 25,000,000 people carried over the years.

During World War II the majority of the few remaining passenger steamers in the Northeast were requisitioned for war duty as hospital ships, troop and freight transports, submarine tenders, and even floating barracks. In 1954 the Eastern Steamship Lines sold off its remaining floating assets and ceased operations altogether on Long Island Sound. Today, only a few small passenger and car ferries continue to operate around the local waters of New England and the Northeast—faint and fading manifestations of this remarkably durable and once essential industry.

Pacific Steamboats

The introduction of steamships into the Pacific lagged far behind their development in the Atlantic coastal and transoceanic trade, for two primary reasons. The first of these was that prior to the late 1840s there were simply too few people along the Pacific coasts of North and South America to support regular steamship service. During this period, the primary maritime industry in the Pacific was the fur, hide and tallow trade in the Northwest, and its modest needs were adequately served by sailing vessels. The other major deterrent was the unavailability in the area of a reliable source of coal, which by this time was becoming the favored fuel for nearly all types of steamships travelling over long distances.

The first steamboat ever to reach the Pacific coast of North America was the *Beaver*, which arrived in 1836, after a 163 day journey from England, where she had been built. This little vessel, measuring 101.4 feet and 109.12 tons, excited great public interest right from the outset; contemporary accounts relate that her launching ceremony was attended by King William and no fewer than 150,000 people. Built specifically by the Hudson's Bay Company to link together its scattered trading outposts in Oregon and British Columbia, the *Beaver* was aptly named; her two 75-horsepower engines consumed up to 50 cords of wood per day. She faithfully served her original and later owners for more than fifty years, carrying general cargo,

Photograph of the *Beaver* in Victoria, British Columbia (PMS Photo No. 21483, Courtesy of the Oregon Historical Society).

Wreck of the *Beaver* off Vancouver Island. She sat on the rocks from 1888 until 1892, when the wake of a passing steamship washed her into deeper water (PMS Photo No. 9744).

passengers and mail in the Pacific Northwest until she was wrecked in 1888 off Vancouver Island.

The factors which hindered the introduction of regular steamship service in the Pacific were forever altered by the discovery of gold at Sutter's Mill in Coloma, California in January 1848, and by similar discoveries a few years later in Australia, Colorado and Nevada respectively. The lure of instant riches was irresistible for hundreds of thousands of people, and by the end of 1848 prospectors were flooding the shipping offices back East trying to secure passage to the gold fields aboard virtually any vessel afloat.

The company best able to fulfill the demands of the gold seekers was the Pacific Mail Steamship Company. Coincidentally, the company had been chartered in New York in April 1848 after winning a government mail contract for service from Panama to Oregon with an annual subsidy of $199,000. The three essentially identical steamers the Pacific Mail Steamship Company built to carry the mails were in a perfect position to carry prospectors as well as the mails, and by the end of 1848 all three vessels, the *California*, *Panama*, and *Oregon*, were in service. Initially, the Pacific Mail Steamship Company provided regular service only from Panama to California, with other steamship lines, such as George Law's United States Mail Steamship Company, providing passage from New York to Panama. For fourteen months the Pacific Mail Steamship Company enjoyed a monopoly on its West Coast run, and rates were accordingly high. Passage from the Isthmus of Panama to San Francisco was normally $300 for cabin passengers and $150 for steerage, but prospectors at the Isthmus, desperate to be among the first to reach El Dorado, paid up to $1,000 to ticket scalpers or passengers with tickets willing to wait a little longer.

At the time, most westward travellers booked passage to the Isthmus at Panama, and were forced to find their own way at their own expense over the approximately 50 miles of Isthmus. Commodore Cornelius Vanderbilt, seeking an alternate route, inaugurated a steamship line bridging the Isthmus at Nicaragua, but he sold out the first of his western steamship lines to the opposition once the Panama Railway was completed in 1855, which cut crossing of the Isthmus to only four hours and essentially put him temporarily out of business. At the height of the gold rush, ships were arriving in San Francisco with up to 1,000 passengers crowded on board.

The revenues of the major steamship lines providing service to the West

The *Goliah* of 1849 was one of the earliest tugboats built in New York, and was sold to a California shipping company during the Gold Rush. This unsigned oil painting shows her passing Tierra Del Fuego in 1850, en route to her new owners (M-11371, F. B. C. Bradlee Collection).

The Pacific Mail Steamship Company's *California* was built in New York in 1848 for mail service between Panama and San Francisco. On her first voyage to San Francisco, the entire crew, excepting only her captain and the third assistant engineer, deserted to join the Gold Rush (M-11317, F. B. C. Bradlee Collection).

U.S. PACIFIC MAIL SHIP CALIFORNIA.

NEW-YORK AND CALIFORNIA STEAMSHIP LINE
VIA NICARAGUA.
THE SHORTEST AND CHEAPEST ROUTE FOR
SAN FRANCISCO.

The Accessory Transit Co. of Nicaragua, Proprietors.

THROUGH IN ADVANCE OF THE MAIL.
Only Line giving Through Tickets, including the Isthmus Crossing.

THE FAVORITE DOUBLE ENGINE STEAMSHIP
STAR OF THE WEST,
CAPT. TINKLEPAUGH, 2,000 TONS BURTHEN, precisely, for SAN JUAN del NORTE, on **FRIDAY, JANUARY 20th 1854,** connecting with the Fast and Favorite Steamship
SIERRA NEVADA,
2,000 Tons burthen, over the NICARAGUA TRANSIT ROUTE, having but TWELVE MILES OF LAND TRANSPORTATION.
These Steamers are unsurpassed in their ventilation and accomodations.
For information or Passage, at the LOWEST RATES, apply only to
CHARLES MORGAN, Agent.
No. 5 Bowling Green, N. Y.
A Mail Bag will be made up at the Office.
BARTRAM's Print, 102 Maiden Lane.

RATES OF PASSAGE.

First Cabin in Deck State Room,.................$275
Do   in Saloon State Room............ ... 250
Second Cabin, open Berth,......................... 175
        STEERAGE.
Upper.. 100
Lower... 90

Including a passage over the Transit Route, from the Atlantic to the Pacific Ocean.

Baggage, 25 lbs. free across Isthmus.
Baggage in Steamship, 250 lbs. free.
Baggage on Transit Route, 15 cts. per lb., over 25 lbs.
Passengers board themselves from one Ship to the other.

Sailing card advertising passage from New York to California via the Isthmus of Nicaragua in 1854. The Accessory Transit Company was owned and operated by "Commodore" Cornelius Vanderbilt; the *Star of the West* was the company's last vessel to sail for the line in 1856 prior to the termination of its charter (Phillips Library).

Coast fluctuated wildly over the next decade or two, waxing from intense competition, additional discoveries of gold in Australia, Colorado and Nevada, and the completion of the Panama Railway, and then waning as various deposits were mined out, and as a result of the opening of the Overland Stage Route in 1858, the Overland Telegraph in 1861, and the Overland Railway in 1869. As a result, steamship traffic from the East through to the West Coast had diminished somewhat by the mid 1860s, and alternate sources of revenue had to be sought and developed.

In 1865 Congress passed legislation authorizing a mail service to China with an annual subsidy of $500,000, in response to increased interest in developing stronger relations with the Orient. Although American steamships had visited China before, the great transoceanic distances involved, the absence of reliable fuel supplies, and the general lack of commercial opportunities had prevented regular service from being developed at an earlier date. As the sole bidder, the Pacific Mail Steamship Company won the mail contract and immediately commissioned four immense wooden paddlewheel

Broadside, ca. 1854, for through service from New York to the West Coast via the U. S. Mail Steamship Company and the Pacific Mail Steamship Company (Phillips Library).

U.S. Mail Steamship Co. { Connecting with the } Pacific Mail Steamship Co.

CARRYING THE GREAT UNITED STATES MAIL.

CALIFORNIA AND OREGON,

VIA ASPINWALL AND PANAMA, DIRECT.

By order of the Postmaster General, the United States Mail Steamers, with the great California and Oregon Mails, are to be dispatched on the 5th and 20th of each month, from New York direct for Aspinwall; and from New Orleans direct for Aspinwall on the 7th and 22d. When these dates occur on Sunday, the sailing to be postponed until the Monday following. The Pacific Mail Steamers are to be in readiness for immediate dispatch on arrival of the Mails at Panama.

The public are informed that the P. M. S. S. Co. always have ONE OR MORE EXTRA STEAMERS laying at Panama, to provide against accidents; and as these facilities are not possessed by any other line, on this or any other route to California, this is the only line that can guarantee through passages without detention.

UNITED STATES MAIL STEAMSHIP COMPANY.

The following is a list of the Steamships belonging to this Company:

ILLINOIS,	2,500 Tons.		UNITED STATES,	1,500 Tons.
GEO. LAW,	2,500 Tons.		CRESCENT CITY,	1,500 Tons.
GEORGIA,	3,000 Tons.		PHILADELPHIA,	1,100 Tons.
OHIO,	3,000 Tons.		EL DORADO,	1,300 Tons.
EMPIRE CITY,	2,000 Tons.		FALCON,	1,000 Tons.

Leaving New York for Aspinwall, from Pier foot of Warren Street, North River, on the 5th and 20th of each month, at 2 P. M.

The new Steamship UNITED STATES and the EL DORADO will form a direct line between NEW ORLEANS and ASPINWALL, leaving on the 7th and 22d of each month, and forming with the Pacific Steamships a through line to and from New Orleans and Ports in Mexico, California and Oregon. Passage from New Orleans can be secured from ARMSTRONG, HARRIS & Co., or JAS. R. JENNINGS, Agents, at that place.

TRANSIT OF THE ISTHMUS.

Passengers are landed at the Panama Railroad Depot, Aspinwall, FREE OF EXPENSE. The Railroad is now in operation, and cars running to Gorgona; the river navigation is avoided; leaving but 21 miles of land travel to Panama. The transit of the Isthmus may be performed in from eighteen to twenty-four hours—the expense, which varies from $10 to $30, to be borne by the passengers.

PACIFIC MAIL STEAMSHIP COMPANY.

The following Steam Packets, belonging to the Pacific Mail Steamship Company, are now on the Pacific, one or more of which will be always in port at each end of the route, to provide against accidents:

J. L. STEPHENS,	2,500 Tons.		PANAMA,	1,087 Tons.
GOLDEN GATE,	2,500 Tons.		CALIFORNIA,	1,050 Tons.
SAN FRANCISCO,	3,000 Tons.		COLUMBIA,	800 Tons.
SACRAMENTO,	2,500 Tons.		CAROLINA,	600 Tons.
NORTHERNER,	1,200 Tons.		COLUMBUS,	600 Tons.
REPUBLIC,	1,200 Tons.		ISTHMUS,	600 Tons.
OREGON,	1,099 Tons.		FREMONT,	600 Tons.

Under the new arrangements of this Company, Steamers inspected and approved by the Navy Department, and carrying the U. S. Mails, will hereafter leave PANAMA immediately on arrival of the Atlantic Mails, and SAN FRANCISCO on the 1st and 16th days of each month, and will touch at ACAPULCO.

The Steamship COLUMBIA will ply between San Francisco and Ports in Oregon, awaiting at the former Port the arrival of the Mails and Passengers from Panama, and returning without delay with the Mails and Passengers for the Steamer from San Francisco. Persons securing through passage by the United States Mail Steamers from New York, have preference of accommodation on board the Pacific Mail Steamers. Children and servants are taken at half price.

An experienced Surgeon is permanently attached to each Steamer in these lines. Each Passenger is allowed 250 lbs. personal baggage free, not exceeding in measurement 10 cubic feet. Freight will be taken to Chagres at 70 cents per foot, and from Panama to San Francisco at the rate of $100 per ton.

FOR FREIGHT OR PASSAGE, APPLY TO

CHARLES A. WHITNEY,

At the Office of the Companies, 177 West Street, corner of Warren Street, NEW YORK.

The *Midas*, built in East Boston in 1844 by Samuel Hall, was the first American steamboat in Chinese waters (M-4964).

steamers to be built for the China run. Essentially sisterships, the *China*, *Great Republic*, *Japan* and *America* measured approximately 360 feet in length by 49 feet across the guards, and 4,000 tons gross. These vessels, already anachronisms at the time of their construction, were nearly the largest commercial steamers ever built of wood, and were among the last oceangoing sidewheelers ever constructed. Part of the reason for their huge size was that they had to carry as much as 2,800 tons of cargo as well as 1,500 tons of coal each way; their 1,500-horsepower engines consumed up to 45 tons of coal per day, and there were no fuel depots along the proposed route to China in the early days of the service. Each had space for 250 cabin passengers and 1,200 in steerage, to accommodate the large numbers of merchants, tourists and Chinese immigrants travelling in both directions. The China run (San Francisco to Yokohama) proved to be a financial success, and the Pacific Mail Steamship Company and its competitors added additional, more modern iron screw steamers to their lines to accommodate additional trade.

Just such a vessel, the *City of Tokio*, carried the famed American naturalist Edward Sylvester Morse, the father of Japanese archaeology, on the first

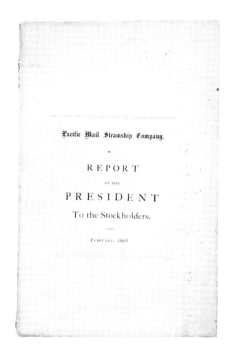

(*Left*) Annual report to the stockholders of the Pacific Mail Steamship Company, 1868 (Phillips Library).

(*Right*) Drawing from diary of Edward Sylvester Morse illustrating the stateroom opposite to his own aboard the *City of Tokio* in 1877 (Phillips Library).

PMSS Co.'s steamship *Great Republic* in the Erie Basin Dry Docks, ca. 1867 (PM Photo No. 11871).

of his several trips to Japan in 1877. The three week voyage between San Francisco and Yokohama was monotonous, and Morse filled his time by recording in his diary his observations of his fellow passengers, their activities, and the ship itself. Today his diary entries offer a most unusual perspective on what contemporary steamship travel was actually like.

During the latter half of the nineteenth century, the steamship business was booming along the Pacific coast from California to Canada and northward to Alaska. Dozens of lines sprang up to accommodate the tremendous volume of seaborne trade resulting from the increased population and commercial activity. Most of the steamboats belonging to these lines were smaller than their eastern counterparts, and they tended to be built after the midwestern river (Mississippi and Ohio systems) paradigm, reflecting the higher proportion of river rather than open water traffic in the area. Although there was considerable prejudice among professional steamboat officers and crews against the sternwheeler along the Mississippi, Missouri and Ohio Rivers, they became quite popular in the Pacific, beginning in the 1870s. Western rivers are generally narrower, shallower and have tighter turns than those in the Midwest, and the shallow draft sternwheelers were better suited to these conditions. Moreover, there were fewer wharves and docks along the western waterways, and sidewheelers tended to ground the inboard paddlewheel when putting into the riverbank. In addition, a single sternwheel paddle was simpler and had fewer moving parts than the double sidewheel steamer; an important factor when critical spare parts often had to be imported from eastern shipyards. Generally, West Coast steamboats tended to be more lightly built than those in the East or the Midwest; an example of this is the slender hogging chain of wire which prevented the western steamers from sagging in the middle, as opposed to the hogging frame of steel or iron prevalent back East.

The same factors that hastened the demise of the steamship in eastern and midwestern waters were at work in the Pacific as well. The development of alternate, more efficient forms of transportation and communications, wartime requisitions, and the Depression all contributed to a gradual reduction of services. By the end of World War II, most of the few remaining passenger steamers in service along the Pacific coast of America had been converted to automobile ferries, and by 1958 the Canadian Pacific Railway was the only operator of passenger steamers along the West Coast.

China Trade items brought to the United States in the late nineteenth century aboard steamships (Top: E-46495, Gift of Esther Oldham; Bottom: M-7055, Gift of Mary and Susan Williams).

The *Bailey Gatzert* of 1890, shown here in the shallow waters of the Columbia River bordering Oregon and Washington, was a popular Pacific Coast excursion sternwheeler (PMS Photo No. 22748).

Typical early twentieth century trans-Pacific steamer, the PMSS Co.'s steamer *Korea* of 1902. Lithograph by Fred Pansing (M-7944).

4/THE ATLANTIC FERRY

Of all of the navigable bodies of water throughout the world, none has played a more critical role in the history of the steamship and its impact upon society than the Atlantic Ocean, linking the Old and New Worlds. In its waters most of the advanced principles of steam navigation were developed, applied and refined, and their effect upon modern culture and society, seen in retrospect, was enormous. As was the case elsewhere, the beginnings of the Atlantic Ferry, the nickname given transatlantic steamship service, were quite modest.

The first steam-powered vessel to cross the Atlantic was the American ship *Savannah*. Converted by a steamboat captain to a steamer while still under construction as a full-rigged ship, in May 1819 the little 98-foot vessel left Savannah, Georgia for Liverpool. Although there were accommodations for 32 people, neither cargo nor paying passengers were aboard during this historic voyage, perhaps as a result of prejudice against the entire idea. The *Savannah*, which only used her engines for about four hours a day, managed to cross to Liverpool in 29 days, but the owner sold her shortly afterwards at a loss, due to lack of business.

Although the sidewheeler *Royal William* crossed the Atlantic under sustained steam power in 1833, and the *Sirius* in 1838, these voyages were little more than isolated incidents. It was not until 1839, when the British government advertised a mail contract for service between Halifax and England with an annual subsidy of £55,000 that regular transatlantic steamship service became a reality. The successful low bidder was the Halifax businessman and shipper Samuel Cunard (1787–1865), who at the age of 51 was about to undertake his greatest and most daring enterprise. Notwithstanding a modest working-class background, Cunard owned his first ship by the age of 21, and a fleet of forty vessels by the onset of the War of 1812. Although he declined an opportunity to invest in a steamship in 1829, he and his brothers were principal backers of the Quebec-built steamer *Royal William*, and later purchased in 1838 the first steam powered Cunard vessel, the

STEAM SHIP "**SAVANNAH**" CAPT. MOSES RODGERS.
THE FIRST STEAMSHIP THAT CROSSED THE ATLANTIC OCEAN

The American steamer *Savannah* is generally credited with having made the first transatlantic passage under steam power, although her engines were in use only part of each day due to the accumulation of salt in her boiler (FLH Pr. 436, Francis Lee Higginson, Jr. Collection).

(*Bottom left*) The *Royal William* of 1833, in which Samuel Cunard and his brothers were investors, was among the first steamers to cross the Atlantic under sustained steam power (M-6440, Charles H. Taylor Collection).

(*Below*) Ship letter dating to 1846 from aboard the *Unicorn* of 1836, the first steamship of the Cunard Line (Phillips Library, Gift of Tracy G. Thurber).

Unicorn. Cunard's extensive shipping background and his fine record in operating a mail service between Halifax, Boston and Bermuda placed him in an excellent position to be awarded the British mail contract, despite his English competitors' vociferous objections that British mails should be carried by British citizens.

After winning the mail contract and an increase in the annual subsidy to £60,000 for extending mail service to Boston, Cunard contracted with the famous Scottish marine engineer and ship builder Robert Napier to construct four steamships, forming a fleet under the cumbersome name of the British and North American Royal Mail Steam Packet Company. The four sidewheelers *Britannia*, *Acadia*, *Caledonia* and *Columbia*, although built in four separate yards, were essentially identical, measuring 207 feet long by

This oil painting of the *Britannia* by Fitz Hugh Lane, depicting Charles Dickens's voyage to America in 1842, is said to have been offered to the Cunard Line by the artist, but was declined since it made steam navigation appear too hazardous (M-19323, Francis Lee Higginson, Jr. Collection).

34.3 feet beam, and 1,156 tons gross. On 4 July 1840, the *Britannia*, flagship of the fleet and its most famous member, set out from Liverpool with 63 passengers for Halifax and Boston. The arrival of the vessel in Boston two weeks later elicited a collective response from the local citizenry equalled by few subsequent events: there was a spontaneous parade of several thousand marchers, a magnificent municipal banquet attended by 2,000 people, and Cunard also received more than 1,800 dinner invitations (and several marriage proposals) as well as an immense silver cup worth $5,000

View of East Boston in 1879, illustrating the wharves of the Cunard Line at the far right and in a vignette in the lower right corner (FLH Pr. 262, Francis Lee Higginson, Jr. Collection).

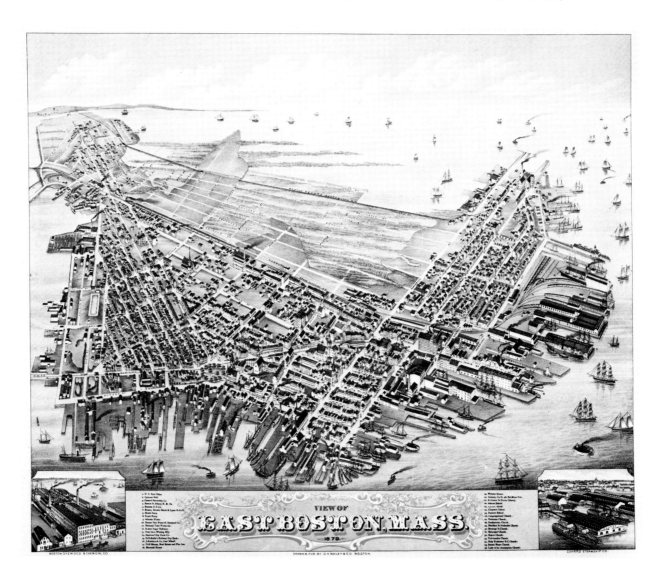

contributed by 2,500 delighted Bostonians. The city of Boston also provided Cunard with a rent-free steamship terminal for a period of twenty
years in gratitude for his choice of their city as his terminus—a wise move,
for duties on the cargo of a single Cunard liner voyage later reached as much
as $100,000.

Speed and safety were the two most important factors in the design of the
Britannia, her sisterships and all subsequent Cunard liners. Luxury was not
at this early date as important as it would shortly become, and at least one
passenger described the conditions aboard the *Britannia* in less than flatter-
ing terms. In January of 1842 the author Charles Dickens and his wife set
out from Liverpool aboard the *Britannia* for their first visit to the United
States. In his book *American Notes*, Dickens described in minute detail his
voyage, beginning with his stateroom, which he described as ". . . this ut-
terly impracticable, thoroughly hopeless and profoundly preposterous box
. . . . [with] two berths, one above the other, than which nothing smaller for
sleeping in was ever made except coffins. . . ." Elaborating upon his funer-
eal imagery, Dickens described the main saloon, which an overzealous Cun-

Vegetable dish of the Cunard Line,
ca 1840–1850, showing the first
four transatlantic Cunard liners
(*Acadia, Britannia, Caledonia, Columbia*) surrounding an image of
one of their ladies' cabins (M-5800,
Gift of Lawrence W. Jenkins).

ard artist had depicted as being "a chamber of almost interminable perspective," as "a long narrow apartment, not unlike a gigantic hearse with windows in the sides. . . ." Returning to Great Britain six months later, Dickens booked passage aboard the sailing ship *George Washington*.

In the early years of the Atlantic Ferry, the Cunard Line had two principal competitors. The earlier of these was The Great Western Steamship Company of Bristol, England which actually antedated the Cunard Line by two years in transatlantic steamship service. The Great Western Steamship Company, a branch of the Great Western Railway, was run by the most famous civil engineer of the nineteenth century, Isambard Kingdom Brunel (1806–1859). Nicknamed "The Little Giant," Brunel built or designed all sorts of projects, ranging from railroads to bridges and tunnels, before turning his attention to steamships in 1835. His first attempt in steam navigation, the *Great Western*, was specifically built to be the first steamer to cross the Atlantic solely under steam power. Although she lost this distinction by only a few hours to the *Sirius* in 1838, Brunel was undaunted, and he moved on to an even more ambitious and radical steam vessel, the *Great Britain*. This steamer incorporated a number of revolutionary concepts, including a propeller drive, an iron hull, wire rigging, hinged masts, a balanced rudder, watertight bulkheads, and a clipper bow. Many of these details were added while the ship was under construction in Bristol, which delayed her launching until 1843. These delays and problems with her engines and propulsion system, followed by a grounding off Ireland that lasted eleven months, forced the company to sell both of its steamships at a great loss, leaving Brunel back where he had started.

Still undiscouraged, however, Brunel formed the Eastern Steam Navigation Company and undertook to build in 1854 his most radical marine engineering project, the steamship *Great Eastern*. Measuring 680 feet long and 18,914 tons gross, the *Great Eastern* was designed to carry 4,000 passengers, 6,000 tons of cargo and enough coal—15,000 tons—for direct non-stop service from England to India and Australia. It took more than $5,000,000 and four years to build the massive vessel, unsurpassed in size for nearly fifty years, and nearly five times larger than any vessel in existence at the time of her construction. Among her most innovative features were a cellular double bottom, a steering engine, and no less than three types of propulsion— sidewheel paddles, propeller and sails. The sheer size of the *Great Eastern*,

Oil painting by Joseph Walter of Brunel's steamship *Great Britain* of 1843, showing her progressively raked masts (FLH 260, Francis Lee Higginson, Jr. Collection).

combined with her radical technology, caused delays which forced Brunel's partner and two subsequent sets of owners into bankruptcy before the vessel was even launched. Moreover, Brunel himself died prior to his greatest vessel's maiden voyage, and without his dynamic and charismatic guidance her third set of owners elected to place her in transatlantic service, where she was a dismal failure. Her only success, aside from serving as a popular pierside tourist attraction in Liverpool and New York, was as a telegraphic cable-laying ship between 1866 and 1873. The *Great Eastern* was subsequently laid up, and although several schemes were suggested for refurbishing her and returning her to service, she served out her last days as a floating billboard for a Liverpool department store chain.

Cunard's other major competitor was the American Edward Knight Col-

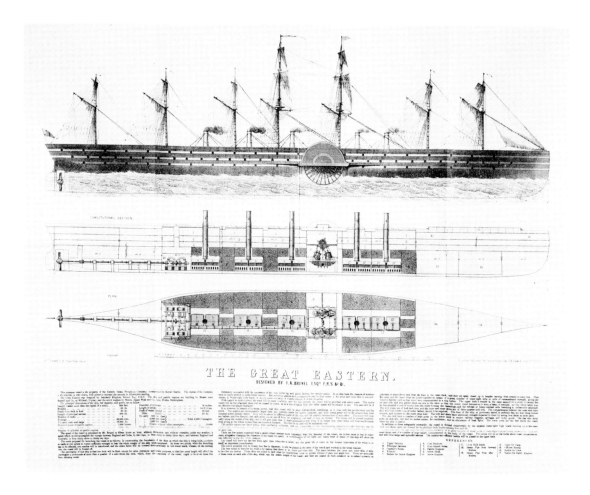

An 1856 lithograph illustrating three views of Brunel's greatest ship, the *Great Eastern*, completed in 1859 (Phillips Library).

lins (1802–1878), owner of the Dramatic Line of transatlantic sailing packets. Recognizing the potential of the steamship as early as 1838, Collins had lobbied the American government to subsidize an American overseas steamship mail service, but not until 1847 did Congress enact legislation in an effort to block the British "monopoly" of steam navigation. The terms of the legislation called for a transatlantic mail contract with an annual subsidy of $385,000, and the construction of five steamships for bimonthly service from New York to Liverpool. Congress also required that the five steamships be of a certain size and speed, so that they might be convertible to wartime duty. Winning the contract, Collins founded the New York and Liverpool United States Mail Steamship Company (also known as the Collins Line) and commissioned the construction of the four sister steamships

Souvenir handkerchief produced by the *Great Eastern*'s last owners, the Lewis department store chain of Liverpool, which used the vessel for publicity purposes (M-4127, Gift of Walter J. Creighton).

Atlantic, Pacific, Arctic and *Baltic*. In keeping with his intention to make his liners the flagships of the American merchant marine, Collins spared no expense in their construction and outfitting. At the time of the inauguration of service in 1850, the Collins liners were the fastest, largest and most magnificiently appointed steamships in the world. Measuring around 283 feet in length by 45 feet over the guards, and 2,783 tons gross, they included such special accoutrements as stained glass skylights and steam heat in the public rooms, bellpulls for steward service in the staterooms, ice houses (to avoid carrying live animals) and 3,500-bottle wine cellars.

From the maiden voyage of the *Atlantic* in April 1851, the Collins liners were an instant success. They were faster and more elegant than Cunard's vessels, and within a year they had won the majority of the American pas-

senger service and had forced Cunard to lower his rates to remain competitive. There was one major problem, however, and that was that the Collins Line was losing money, especially during the winter months when passenger revenues declined. Collins wined, dined and lobbied federal officials for additional funding, and in a fit of patriotic zeal Congress increased his annual subsidy to $858,000 in early 1853. This fiscal windfall, combined with the requisitioning by the British government of much of the British merchant fleet for Crimean War service, served to create an artificially sound economic climate for the Collins Line over the next eighteen months. The situation began to change, however, in the fall of 1854, when the Collins liner *Arctic* collided with another steamer off Newfoundland. Although it was foggy the afternoon of 27 September 1854 when the collision occurred, the *Arctic* was proceeding at full speed, to maintain the Collins Line's reputation for the swiftest passages. Of the 432 crew and passengers aboard the *Arctic*, 348 were lost, including Collins' wife and two children. In early 1856

Oil painting by Samuel Walters depicting the departure from England of Jenny Lind, the Swedish Nightingale, 21 August 1850. She came to America aboard the Collins liner *Atlantic* for a tour organized by P. T. Barnum (FLH 285, Francis Lee Higginson, Jr. Collection).

LOSS OF THE U.S.M. STEAM SHIP ARCTIC,

another Collins liner, the *Pacific*, departed from Liverpool with some 150 passengers bound for New York, and was never seen again. Individually, these two disasters had little material effect upon the operations of the Collins Line, but together they proved devastating. There was a public outcry against the line for operating in dangerous waters at unsafe speeds, and Collins encountered difficulty maintaining his regular sailing schedules with two liners lost. Passengers flocked in record numbers to the Cunard Line, which had never lost a passenger. In August of 1856 Congress cut Collins' subsidy to the original $385,000 and within a few months service began to decline. Despite the addition of the fast new steamship *Adriatic* in late 1857, the Collins Line never did recover, and it ceased operations in February 1858, the victim of bad luck and poor management. It did, however, set the standards of speed and luxury for transatlantic liners, which along with safety were to remain the three most important factors in steamship design for the next century.

Popular Currier lithograph depicting the wreck of the Collins liner *Arctic*, 27 September 1854 (M-11300, F. B. C. Bradlee Collection).

The Blue Riband of the Atlantic

Collins had proved that one of the best drawing cards for his line was to offer the fastest transatlantic passage possible. Within a few years, all of the major transatlantic steamship lines, including the conservative Cunard Line, were ordering progressively swifter vessels, and an informal rivalry resulted, called the Blue Riband of the Atlantic. Although the competition was officially denied by the steamship lines, and denounced by the press as reckless and unsafe, the public loved it, and whatever ship held the Blue Riband at any given moment was assured a spot on the front pages of the major European and American newspapers, as well as a full complement of passengers and freight.

With the exception of the American Collins liners of the 1850s, the Blue Riband competition was dominated by the major British shipping companies until the end of the nineteenth century, with the lead changing hands frequently between the Cunard, Inman, White Star, Guion and National Lines. The flagships of these Liverpool-based lines gradually became larger in order to remain profitable, and swifter and more luxurious in order to remain competitive. As a result, this period, the latter half of the nineteenth century, saw major breakthroughs in ship design and propulsion systems technology, with such fundamental alterations as the changeover from wooden to iron and then steel hulls, from sidewheel paddles to propellers, and from compound engines to turbines.

In 1897 the German Norddeutscher Lloyd Line entered the competition with its new steamship *Kaiser Wilhelm der Grosse*, which broke the British monopoly of the Blue Riband. Both Norddeutscher Lloyd and the associated Hamburg Amerika Line from 1857 had concentrated upon the emigrant trade between Bremen and New York, and in fact during the decade between 1881 and 1891 had together transported more passengers to America than the White Star, Cunard, Inman and Guion Lines combined. The *Kaiser Wilhelm der Grosse* was NDL's attempt to upgrade both its aging fleet as well as its prestige, and before the end of 1897 the ship had achieved the distinction of being the fastest and largest steamship in transatlantic service. NDL retained the Blue Riband until the British government, concerned by the loss of its maritime prestige and the impending threat of an immense American steamship combine organized by J. Pierpont Morgan, subsidized

Oil painting attributed to Fred Pansing of the Inman liner *City of Paris II*. This vessel, whose clipper bow, cutaway stern and sharply raked masts and funnels imply great speed, held the Blue Riband in 1889 for the fastest eastward and westward passages between Liverpool and New York (M-11406, F. B. C. Bradlee Collection).

The *Kaiser Wilhelm der Grosse* of the Norddeutscher Lloyd Line broke the British monopoly on the Blue Riband by winning it for the German shipping company in late 1897 (PMS Photo No. 22764).

Cunard's *Mauretania* in World War I camouflage, called "dazzle paint." This modernistic design was intended to prevent enemy ships from determining in what direction a vessel was travelling (PMS Photo No. 22765).

After the flood of immigrants slowed in the early 1920s, the major transatlantic steamship lines concentrated upon luxurious accommodations for tourists, as illustrated by this Cabin Class suite aboard the NDL Blue Riband liner *Bremen* of 1929 (PMS Photo No. 22766).

the Cunard Line in the construction of two of its most famous sisterships, the *Lusitania* and *Mauretania*, launched in 1906. The pair were specifically designed to attain 24.5 knots, which they both exceeded by means of four propellers driven by some of the earliest steam turbines installed in ocean liners. Due to minor engineering differences the *Mauretania* was marginally faster than her ill-fated sibling *Lusitania*, and broke all existing speed records, including some as late as 1929. Once again Britain ruled the waves.

Within the next decade, however, several different nations subsidized their countries' major lines in the construction of contenders for the Blue Riband, all of which held the coveted prize at one time or another. Norddeutscher Lloyd's *Bremen* (1929) and *Europa* (1930), the Italian Line's *Rex* (1932), the French Line's *Normandie* (1935) and Cunard's *Queen Mary* (1936)—all carried their nations' standards in times of peace and war, serving as fleet and magnificent monuments to national pride and patriotism. These great liners and their slower but no less distinguished sisters, all built after restrictive immigration legislation was passed by the United States government in 1921 and 1924, represented the epitome of modern steamship transportation and all it embodied: outright speed, gracious luxury, elegant service and sheer overwhelming scale.

Only one liner ever exceeded the record set by the *Queen Mary* in 1938. This was the largest liner ever built in America, the *United States*, designed by Gibbs and Cox, Inc. of New York. Launched in 1951 during the Korean War, the *United States* was specifically designed as a passenger liner capable of carrying 14,000 troops in wartime, and on her maiden voyage overseas she set both eastward and westward records, averaging slightly over 35 knots (40.3 mph). The *United States* served as the flagship of the American merchant marine until 1969, when she was laid up as uneconomical. In the expectation that no passenger liner would ever exceed her transatlantic speed record, the Hales Blue Riband trophy, a magnificent cup commissioned by the Briton Harold Hales in 1935 and given to holders of the Blue Riband, was retired along with the *United States*.

Today these great transatlantic passenger liners exist only as memories. The Cunard Line's *Queen Elizabeth 2* is alone in offering occasional transatlantic passages, but only in the summer months. During the remainder of the year, she and the other remaining passenger ships are limited to short cruises in the Caribbean and elsewhere. *QE 2*'s namesake, Cunard's *Queen*

(*Top*) Oil painting by Jack L. Gray of Cunard's best known ocean liner of the twentieth century, the Blue Ribander *Queen Mary* of 1936 (FLH 140, Francis Lee Higginson, Jr. Collection).

(*Left*) The *United States* of 1952, the fastest passenger liner ever built, depicted during her speed trials. Her top speed, which is still secret, is said to have been 42 knots (48.36 mph), although the vibration at this speed was reputedly so great that it was difficult to stand upright in the engine room (PMS Photo No. 20170, Courtesy of Wide World Photo).

Elizabeth, was broken up in the mid 1970s after rusting for years on her side in Hong Kong harbor, the victim of a fire, while her sistership, the *Queen Mary*, serves out her days as an in-water tourist attraction alongside a wharf in Long Beach, California. The *United States* lies mothballed in Newport News, Virginia; although occasionally plans are made to refit her and place her back in service, this seems unlikely in view of the prohibitive costs, recently estimated at more than $35,000,000.

Retired by economic circumstances and superseded by passenger jets, the great steamships, along with the era they represent, are no more. Their impact upon human culture, so critical in the nineteenth and early twentieth centuries, has been largely relegated to studies in historical books and journals, the regrettable though perhaps inevitable fate for nearly all anachronisms in modern society.

In service as a troop ship during World War II, the French Line steamship *Normandie* caught fire in New York harbor in November 1942. Firemen pumped so much water into her that she capsized from the weight of the water, much of which froze. Although refloated, she was never again put into service (PMS Photo No. 19568, Gift of Parker H. Kemble).

APPENDIX

The Steamship Collections in the Peabody Museum

The Peabody Museum of Salem has one of the most extensive collections of steamship-related materials in the world. The collection comprises several different categories of resources; the numbers supplied are approximate, and are intended only to serve as a general guide to the relative size of each category. The brief outline below includes only materials associated with commercial steamships, and omits yachts, naval and fishing vessels propelled by steam.

Paintings and drawings

More than 310 original works, including oils, watercolors, pen and ink sketches and drawings. The subject matter ranges in date from the *Fulton* of 1813 to the container ship *Carrier* of 1970, but focuses primarily on transatlantic and New England steamships from the mid-nineteenth through the early twentieth century. Alphabetically indexed by artist and ship's name, if known.

Prints and posters

Approximately 800 steamship engravings, broadsides, prints and posters, ranging in date of subject matter from the late eighteenth century to the present. The major concentration is transatlantic and New England steamships from the mid-nineteenth through the early twentieth century. Alphabetically indexed by shipping company or ship's name, if known.

Ship Models

Approximately 63 models of commercial steamships, from the *Fulton* of 1813 to the *Queen Elizabeth* of 1938, with the majority comprising transat-

The first American stamp with a steamship was issued in 1869, and displayed an image of the last Collins liner, the *Adriatic* (Phillips Library, Osgood Williams Collection).

lantic passenger liners from the mid-nineteenth through the early twentieth century. Included are cargo vessels, tankers, liners, ferries, tugboats, and English Channel steamers, in the form of builders', plating and designers' models (half and full hull), display, teaching, toy and souvenir models. Alphabetically indexed by ship's name if known; otherwise by date.

Plans

Approximately 1000 sheets of steamship plans, primarily of vessels built in New England and the Northeast in the late nineteenth and early twentieth centuries. Blueprints, blackprints, tracings, photographs, linens and vellums of hulls, engines, boilers, propulsion and special systems, deck plans and elevations. Some 354 of the sheets are alphabetically indexed by ship's name; the remainder are identified by ship type, hull or job number.

Photographs

Approximately 200,000 photographic images of steamships of all types and geographic locations, in subject matter dating from the mid-nineteenth century to the present. Included are photographs, prints, stereographs, postcards, glass plate, nitrate and safety film negatives (many unprinted).

Appendix

Indexed by nationality, shipping line and ship's name (respectively), if known.

Phillips Library manuscripts, documents and archives

Several thousand individual steamship-related items, ranging in date from the early nineteenth century to the present. Many different categories of materials, including logbooks, diaries, journals, letters, newspapers, bills of sale, shipping records and contracts, certificates of association, tickets, broadsides, sailing cards and schedules, advertising brochures, books and pamphlets, deck and berth plans, menus, sheet music and sheet music covers, shipping company letterheads, philately, and miscellaneous items. Arranged by geographic location, shipping company, ship's name, or category of collection.

Memorabilia

Approximately 500 steamship-related items, dating from the early nineteenth century to the present, including such categories as coins, tokens, medals, medallions, ticket plates, life preservers, flags and pennants, deck lights, engine and bridge gauges, builders' and engine plates, tableware (china and flatware), wooden relics (nameboards, trailboards, paddlebox carvings, figurehead and hull fragments, sections of rail and molding, blocks, sheaves), saloon, stateroom and deck furniture, commemorative and souvenir items (purses, compass cards, hats, handkerchiefs, match boxes, cigarette and cigar lighters, ash trays), buttons, towels, calendars and miscellaneous items. Alphabetically indexed by name of shipping company, ship or associated individual (if known), otherwise by date.

BIBLIOGRAPHY

General and Reference

Albion, R. G. *Naval and Maritime History: An Annotated Bibliography.* 4th rev. ed. Mystic, CT: Munson Institute of American Maritime History and The Marine Historical Association, 1972.

The American Neptune: A Quarterly Journal of Maritime History, 1941–   . American Neptune, Inc., Peabody Museum, Salem, MA.

Bone, D. W. *The Lookoutman.* New York: Harcourt, Brace & Co., 1923.

Bowen, F. C. *Merchant Ships of the World, 1929.* London: S. Low, Marston & Co., 1929.

Buchanan, L. *Ships of Steam.* New York: McGraw-Hill, 1956.

Chatterton, E. K. *Steamships and Their Story.* London: Cassell & Co., 1910.

Dayton, F. E. *Steamboat Days.* New York: Frederick A. Stokes Co., 1928.

Dollar, R. *One Hundred Thirty Years of Steam Navigation: A History of the Merchant Ship.* San Francisco: Schwabacher-Frey Co., 1931.

Dunn, L. *Ships: A Picture History.* London: Pan Books, 1971.

Fletcher, R. A. *Steam-Ships: The Story of Their Development to the Present Day.* Philadelphia: J. B. Lippincott Co., 1910.

Gray, L. *Eighty-Five Years of Shipping Under the Maltese Cross, 1881–1966: Portrait of a Major German Shipping Company.* Kendal, England: World Ship Society, 1967.

Hilton, G. W. *The Illustrated History of Paddle Steamers.* New York: Two Continents, 1976.

Hindle, B. *Emulation and Invention.* New York: New York University Press, 1981.

Hornstein, A. von. *Schiffe and Schiffahrt.* Bern: Verlag Hallwag, 1964.

Jackson, G. G. *The Book of the Ship.* New York: R. M. McBride & Co., 1930.

Jackson, G. G. *The Ship Under Steam.* New York: C. Scribner's Sons, 1928.

Kludas, A. *Great Passenger Ships of the World.* Translated by C. Hodges. 5 vols. Cambridge: Patrick Stephens, 1975.

Leigh-Bennett, E. P. *History of a House Flag.* Rotterdam: W. Ruys & Zonen, 1939.

Lloyd's Register of Shipping. London: Wyman & Son, 1764–   .

Macfarlane, R. *History of Propellers and Steam Navigation with Biographical Sketches of the Early Inventors.* New York: G. P. Putnam, 1851.

McNulty, P., and Schultz, C. R. *Bibliography of Periodical Articles on Maritime and Naval History Published in 1971.* Mystic, CT: Marine Historical Association, 1972.

Murray, R. *Steam-Ships.* 2d ed. Edinburgh: A. and C. Black, 1863.

Plowden, D. *Farewell to Steam.* Brattleboro, VT: S. Greene Press, 1966.

Preble, G. H. *A Chronological History of the Origin and Development of Steam Navigation.* 2d rev. ed. Philadelphia: L. R. Hamersly & Co., 1895.

———. *Notes for a History of Steam Navigation.* Philadelphia: J. B. Lippincott & Co., 1881.

Rainey, T. *Ocean Steam Navigation and the Ocean Post.* 1858. Reprint. New Haven, CT: Eastern Press, 1977.

Rowland, K. T. *Steam at Sea: A History of Steam Navigation.* New York: Praeger Publishers, 1970.

Schultz, C. R. *Bibliography of Maritime and Naval History Periodical Articles During 1970.* Mystic, CT: Marine Historical Association, 1971.

———. *Bibliography of Maritime and Naval History Periodical Articles Published 1972–1973.* College Station, TX: Texas A & M University, 1974.

Smith, E. W. *Passenger Ships of the World, Past and Present.* 2d rev. ed. Boston: George H. Dean Co., 1978.

Spratt, H. P. *The Birth of the Steamboat.* London: C. Griffin & Co., 1958.

Steamboat Bill, quarterly, 1939–   . Steamship Historical Society of America, Staten Island, NY.

Talbot-Booth, E. C. *A Cruising Companion: Ships and the Sea.* New York: D. Appleton-Century Co., 1936.

Williams, D. L., and de Kerbrech, R. P. *Damned by Destiny.* Brighton: Teredo Books, 1982.

Bibliography

General, American

Albion, R. G. *Seaports South of Sahara: The Achievements of an American Steamship Service.* New York: Appleton-Century-Crofts, 1959.

American Steamships, 1807 to 1946. Newport News, VA: Mariners Museum, 1947.

Braynard, F. O. *Famous American Ships.* 2d rev. ed. New York: Hastings House, 1978.

Church, W. C. *The Life of John Ericsson.* New York: C. Scribner's Sons, 1911.

Eskew, G. L. *The Pageant of the Packets: A Book of American Steamboating.* New York: H. Holt, 1929.

Farrell, J. A., Jr. *Sea Lanes South of Sahara: The Story of Farrell Lines, Incorporated.* New York: Newcomen Society of North America, 1963.

Fitch, J. *The Autobiography of John Fitch.* Edited by F. D. Prager. Philadelphia: American Philosophical Society, 1976.

Flexner, J. T. *Steamboats Come True: American Inventors in Action.* 2d ed. Boston: Little, Brown & Co., 1978.

Hall, E. H. *Hudson and Fulton: A Brief History of Henry Hudson and Robert Fulton.* 2d ed. New York: Hudson-Fulton Celebration Commission, 1909.

Heyl, E. *Early American Steamers.* 6 vols. Buffalo, NY: Erick Heyl, 1953–67.

Howland, S. A. *Steamboat Disasters and Railroad Accidents in the United States.* Worcester, MA: Dorr, Howland & Co., 1840.

King, T. *From the Potomac to the Thames: Being the Progress of One James Rumsey (1743–1792).* New York: Newcomen Society, American Branch, 1943.

Knox, T. W. *The Life of Robert Fulton and a History of Steam Navigation.* New York: G. P. Putnam's Sons, 1886.

Lane, C. D. *American Paddle Steamboats.* New York: Coward-McCann, 1943.

Lytle, W. M., and Holdcamper, F. R. *Merchant Steam Vessels of the United States, 1790–1868: "The Lytle-Holdcamper List."* Revised and edited by C. B. Mitchell and K. R. Hall. Staten Island, NY: Steamship Historical Society of America. 1975.

Marestier, J. B. *Memoir on Steamboats of the United States of America.* Paris: 1824. Reprint, translated by S. Withington. Mystic, CT: Marine Historical Association, 1957.

Morrison, J. H. *History of American Steam Navigation.* 2d ed. New York: Stephen Daye Press, 1958.

Stanton, S. W. *American Steam Vessels.* New York: Smith & Stanton, 1895.

Stuart, C. B. *The Naval and Mail Steamers of the United States.* New York: C. B. Norton, 1853.

Virginskii, V. S. *Robert Fulton, 1765–1815.* Translated from Russian. Washington, D.C.: Smithsonian Institution, 1976.

Whittemore, H. *Origin and Progress of American Inventions and American Industries: Part I — Steam Navigation.* New York: Original and Progressive Publishing Co., 1890.

General, British Commonwealth

Brady, H. W. *The Aaron Manby of 1822: New Light on the First Iron Steamer.* Mystic, CT: Steamship Historical Society of America, 1954.

Chandler, G. *Liverpool Shipping: A Short History.* London: Phoenix House, 1960.

Clegg, W. P., and Styring, J. S. *Steamers of British Railways and Associated Companies.* Prescot, England: T. Stephenson, 1962.

Coates, W. H. *The Good Old Days of Shipping.* Bombay: Times of India Press, 1900.

Course, A. G. *Ships of the P and O.* London: A. Coles, 1954.

Crowdy, M. *Lyle Shipping Company Limited, 1827–1966: The Firm and the Fleet.* Kendal, England: World Ship Society, 1966.

Dunn, L. *Ships of the Union-Castle Line.* London: A. Coles, 1954.

Farr, G. E. *West Country Passenger Steamers.* London: R. Tilling, 1956.

Greenhill, B., and Grifford, A. *Victorian and Edwardian Merchant Steamships from Old Photographs.* Annapolis: Naval Institute Press, 1979.

Gregory, C. D. *Australian Steamships Past and Present.* London: Richards Press, 1928.

———. *The Romance of the* Edina, *the World's Oldest Screw-Steamship.* Melbourne: Robertson & Mullens, 1935.

Hambleton, F. C. *Famous Paddle Steamers.* London: P. Marshall & Co., 1948.

Kennedy, N. W., comp. *Records of the Early British Steamships.* Liverpool: C. Birchall & Sons, 1933.

Bibliography

Laxon, W. A. *Asiatic Steam Navigation Company, Limited, 1878–1963*. Kendal, England: World Ship Society, 1963.

Maber, J. M. *North Star to Southern Cross*. Prescot, England: T. Stephenson, 1967.

McLachlan, G. W. P. *Famous Liners of the Eastern Ocean*. London: S. Low, Marston & Co., n.d.

The New Zealand Shipping Company's Pocketbook. London: A. & C. Black, 1908.

Paget-Tomlinson, E. W. *Bibby Line: 175 Years of Achievement*. Liverpool: Bibby Line, 1982.

Stammers, M. K. *The Passage Makers: The History of the Black Ball Line*. Brighton: Teredo Books, 1978.

Talbot-Booth, E. C. *Ships of the British Merchant Navy: Passenger Lines*. London: A. Melrose, 1932.

Thornley, F. C. *Steamers of North Wales, Past and Present*. 2d rev. ed. Prescot, England: T. Stephenson, 1962.

Thornton, E. C. B. *South Coast Pleasure Steamers*. Prescot, England: T. Stephenson, 1962.

American East Coast (including Hudson River)

Borden, P. D. *Steamboating on Narragansett Bay*. West Barrington, RI: Steamship Historical Society of America, 1957.

Bradlee, F. B. C. *Some Account of Steam Navigation in New England*. Salem, MA: Essex Institute, 1920.

Brown, A. C. *The Old Bay Line, 1840–1940*. Richmond, VA: Dietz Press, 1940.

———. *Paddle Box Decorations of American Sound Steamboats*. Newport News, VA: Mariners Museum, 1943.

———. *Steam Packets on the Chesapeake: A History of the Old Bay Line Since 1840*. Cambridge, MD: Cornell Maritime Press, 1961.

Buckman, D. L. *Old Steamboat Days on the Hudson River: Tales and Reminiscences of the Stirring Times That Followed the Introduction of Steam Navigation*. New York: Grafton Press, 1907.

Burgess, R. H., and Wood, H. G. *Steamboats Out of Baltimore*. Cambridge, MD: Tidewater Publishers, 1968.

Covell, W. K. *A Short History of the Fall River Line*. Newport, RI: A. Hartley G. Ward, 1947.

Cram, W. B. *Picture History of New England Passenger Vessels*. Hampden Highlands, ME: Burntcoat Publishers, 1980.

Dow, C. H. *History of Steam Navigation Between New York and Providence from 1792 to 1877*. New York: Wm. Turner & Co., n.d.

Dunbaugh, E. L. *The Era of the Joy Line: A Saga of Steamboating on Long Island Sound*. Westport, CT: Greenwood Press, 1982.

Dunn, W. *Casco Bay Steamboat Album*. Camden, ME: Down East Enterprise, 1969.

Elliott, R. V. *Last of the Steamboats: The Saga of the Wilson Line*. Cambridge, MD: Tidewater Publishers, 1970.

Emmerson, J. C., comp. *Steam Navigation in Virginia and Northeastern North Carolina Waters, 1826–1836*. Compiled from the files of the Norfolk & Portsmouth Herald and the American Beacon. Portsmouth, VA: n.p., 1950.

Hains, J. W. *Side Wheel Steamers of the Chesapeake Bay, 1880–1947*. Glen Burnie, MD: Glendale Press, 1947.

Hill, R. N. *Sidewheeler Saga: A Chronicle of Steamboating*. New York: Rinehart, 1953.

History of Boston and Bangor Steamship Company, Formerly Known as Stanford's Independent Line. Boston: T. R. Marvin & Son, 1882.

Jacobus, M. W. *The Connecticut River Steamboat Story*. Hartford, CT: Connecticut Historical Society, 1956.

Lang, C. R. *Kennebec-Boothbay Harbor Steamboat Album*. Camden, ME: Down East Enterprise, 1971.

McAdam, R. W. *The Old Fall River Line*. 2d rev. ed. New York: Stephen Daye Press, 1955.

———. *Salts of the Sound: An Informal History of Steamboat Days and the Famous Skippers Who Sailed Long Island Sound*. Rev. and enl. New York: Stephen Daye Press, 1957.

Morris, P. C., and Morin, J. F. *The Island Steamers: A Chronology of Steam Transportation to and from the Offshore Islands of Martha's Vineyard and Nantucket*. Nantucket, MA: Nantucket Nautical Publishers, 1977.

Richardson, J. M. *Steamboating Lore of the Penobscot: An Informal Story of Steamboating in Maine's Penobscot Region*. Augusta, ME: Kennebec Journal Print Shop, 1950.

Ringwald, D. C. *Hudson River Day Line: The Story of a Great American Steamboat Company*. Berkeley, CA: Howell-North Books, 1965.

Bibliography

———. *Steamboats for Rondout: Passenger Service Between New York and Rondout Creek, 1829 through 1863*. Providence, RI: Steamship Historical Society of America, 1981.

Ryan, A. *Penobscot Bay, Mount Desert and Eastport Steamboat Album*. Camden, ME: Down East Enterprise, 1972.

Short, V., and Sears, E. *Sail and Steam Along the Maine Coast*. Portland, ME: Bond Wheelwright Co., 1955.

Taylor, W. L. *A Productive Monopoly: The Effect of Railroad Control on New England Coastal Steamship Lines, 1870–1916*. Providence, RI: Brown University Press, 1970.

Turner, H. B. *The Story of the Island Steamers*. Nantucket, MA: Inquirer & Mirror Press, 1910.

American Inland Waters (lakes and midwestern rivers)

Anthony, I. *Paddle Wheels and Pistols*. New York: Grosset & Dunlap, 1929.

Barkhau, R. L. *A History of the Eagle Packet Company*. No imprint.

Blackstone, E. H. *Farewell Old Mount Washington: The Story of the Steamboat Era on Lake Winnipesaukee*. Staten Island, NY: Steamship Historical Society of America, 1969.

Blaisdell, P. H. *Three Centuries on Winnipesaukee*. Concord, NH: Rumford Press, 1936.

Bugbee, G. P. *The Lake Erie Sidewheel Steamers of Frank E. Kirby*. Detroit: Great Lakes Model Shipbuilders' Guild, 1955.

Burman, B. L. *Look Down that Winding River: An Informal Profile of the Mississippi*. New York: Taplinger Publishing Co., 1973.

Chittenden, H. M. *History of Early Steamboat Navigation on the Missouri River: Life and Adventures of Joseph LaBarge*. New York: F. P. Harper, 1903.

Clemens, S. L. [Mark Twain]. *Life on the Mississippi*. New York: Harper & Brothers, 1927.

Coutant, F. R. *Yankee Steamboats on the Fraser River, British Columbia*. Monroe, CT: Frank R. Coutant, 1965.

Curwood, J. O. *The Great Lakes*. New York: G. P. Putnam's Sons, 1909.

Donovan, F. *River Boats of America*. New York: Thomas Y. Crowell, 1966.

Elliott, J. L. *Red Stacks Over the Horizon: The Story of the Goodrich Steamboat Line*. Grand Rapids: Eerdmans, 1967.

Ferber, E. *Showboat*. Garden City, NJ: Doubleday, 1962.

Hilton, G. W. *The Great Lakes Car Ferries*. Berkeley, CA: Howell-North, 1962.

Holden, T. L., and Knight, R. W. *The Songo River Steamboats*. Portland, ME: Anthoenson Press, 1964.

Huber, L. V. *Advertisements of Lower Mississippi River Steamboats 1812–1920*. West Barrington, RI: Steamship Historical Society of America, 1959.

Hult, R. E. *Steamboats in the Timber*. Caldwell, ID: Caxton Printers, 1952.

Lass, W. E. *A History of Steamboating on the Upper Missouri River*. Lincoln, NE: University of Nebraska Press, 1962.

Latrobe, J. H. B. *The First Steamboat Voyage on the Western Waters*. Baltimore: Maryland Historical Society, 1871.

Manse, T. *Know Your Ships*. Sault St. Marie, MI: Thomas Manse, 1960.

Mills, J. C. *Our Inland Seas: Their Shipping and Commerce for Three Centuries*. 1910. Reprint. Cleveland: Freshwater Press, 1976.

Petsche, J. E. *The Steamboat Bertrand: History, Excavation, and Architecture*. Washington, D.C.: National Park Service, 1974.

Quick, H., and Quick, E. *Mississippi Steamboatin': A History of Steamboating on the Mississippi and its Tributaries*. New York: H. Holt & Co., 1926.

Ross, O. J., comp. *The Steamboats of Lake Champlain, 1809 to 1930*. Albany: Champlain Transportation Co., 1930.

The Steamboats of Lake George, 1817 to 1932. Albany: Lake George Steamboat Company, 1932.

Steamboats on the Mississippi. New York: American Heritage Publishing Co., 1962.

Way, F. *The Log of the Betsy Ann*. New York: R. M. McBride & Co., 1933.

———. *Mississippi Stern-Wheelers*. Milwaukee: Kalmbach Publishing Co., 1947.

———. *Pilotin' Comes Natural*. New York: Farrar & Rinehart, 1943.

Wilterding, J. H., Jr. *McDougall's Dream: The American Whaleback*. Green Bay: Lakeside Publications, 1969.

Young, A. E., comp. *The Two Soos, American and Canadian*. Grand Rapids: J. Bayne Co., n.d.

84

Bibliography

American West Coast & Pacific Ocean

Benson, R. M. *Steamships and Motorships of the West Coast*. New York: Bonanza Books, 1968.

Bockstoce, J. R. *Steam Whaling in the Western Arctic*. New Bedford: Old Dartmouth Historical Society, 1977.

Chen, G. *Tseng Kuo-Fan, Pioneer of the Steamship in China*. New York: Paragon Book Reprint, 1968.

Duckworth, C. L. D., and Langmuir, G. E. *West Coast Steamers*. 3rd ed. Prescot, England: T. Stephenson, 1966.

Forbes, R. B. *On the Establishment of a Line of Mail Steamers from the Western Coast of the United States on the Pacific to China*. Boston: Boston Journal Office, 1855.

Heberer, H. M. *A History of Williams, Dimond and Company, 1862–1974*. San Francisco: Williams, Dimond & Co., 1975.

Kemble, J. H., ed. *Gold Rush Steamers*. San Francisco: Book Club of California, 1958.

———. *Side-Wheelers Across the Pacific*. San Francisco: San Francisco Museum of Science and Industry, 1942.

Lawson, W. *Pacific Steamers*. Glasgow: Brown, Son & Ferguson, 1927.

LeFleming, H. M. *Ships of the Blue Funnel Line*. Southampton, England: A. Coles, 1961.

MacMullen, J. *Paddle-Wheel Days in California*. Palo Alto, CA: Stanford University Press, 1944.

Mills, R. V. *Stern-Wheelers Up Columbia: A Century of Steamboating in the Oregon Country*. Palo Alto, CA: Pacific Books, 1947.

Musk, G. *Canadian Pacific Afloat, 1883–1968: A Short History and Fleet List*. 2d rev. ed. Warrington, England: Canadian Pacific, 1968.

Newell, G. R. *Pacific Steamboats*. Seattle: Superior Publishing Co., 1958.

———. *Pacific Tugboats*. Seattle: Superior Publishing Co., 1957.

Newell, G. R., and Williamson, J. *Pacific Coastal Liners*. Seattle: Superior Publishing Co., 1959.

Rasmussen, L. J. *San Francisco Ship Passenger Lists*. 4 vols. Colma, CA: San Francisco Historic Record & Geneaology Bulletin, 1965–1970.

Rushton, G. A. *Whistle Up the Inlet: The Union Steamship Story*. Vancouver: J. J. Douglas, 1974.

Somner, G. *Ben Line: Fleet List and Short History*. Kendal, England: World Ship Society, 1967.

Stewart, C., ed. *Ships of the Orient Line*. London: A. Coles, 1954.

Turner, R. D. *The Pacific Princesses: An Illustrated History of Canadian Pacific Railway's Princess Fleet on the Northwest Coast*. Victoria, B.C.: Sono Nis Press, 1977.

Wardle, A. C. *Steam Conquers the Pacific: A Record of Maritime Achievement, 1840–1940*. London: Hodder and Stoughton, 1940.

Wiltsie, E. A. *Gold Rush Steamers of the Pacific*. 1938. Reprint. Lawrence, MA: Quarterman Publications, 1976.

Wright, E. W., ed. *Lewis and Dryden's Marine History of the Pacific Northwest*. Portland, OR: Lewis & Dryden Print Co., 1895.

The Atlantic Ferry

Anderson, R. *White Star*. Prescot, England: T. Stephenson, 1964.

Appleton, T. E. *Ravenscrag: The Allan Royal Mail Line*. Toronto: McClelland & Stewart, 1974.

Argyle, E. W. *Passenger Liners*. Chippenham, England: Picton Publishing, 1970.

Babcock, F. L. *Spanning the Atlantic*. New York: A. A. Knopf, 1931.

Banks, D. *The Clyde Steamers*. Edinburgh: Albyn Press, 1950.

Barbance, M. *Histoire de la Compagnie Générale Transatlantique: Un Siècle d' Exploitation Maritime*. Paris: Arts et Métiers Graphiques, 1955.

Bennett, W. E. [Warren Armstrong]. *Atlantic Bridge, from Sail to Steam to Wings: A Diverse Record of One Hundred Years of North Atlantic Travel*. London: Muller, 1956.

———. [Warren Armstrong]. *The Collins Story*. London: R. Hale, 1957.

Bonsor, N. R. P. *North Atlantic Seaway: An Illustrated History of the Passenger Services Linking the Old World with the New*. 4 vols. 2d rev. ed. Jersey, Channel Islands: Brookside Publications, 1975.

The Book of the Anchor Line: An Outline of the Company's Activities and Progress from Its Inception in 1852 Until the End of 1931. London: E. J. Burrow & Co., 1932.

Bowen, F. C. *A Century of Atlantic Travel, 1830–1930*. London: S. Low, Marston & Co., 1930.

Braynard, F. O. *Copper for the* Savannah *of 1818*. Philadelphia: Press of M. Jacobs, 1959.

———. *Lives of the Liners*. New York: Cornell Maritime Press, 1947.

Bibliography

———. *S.S.* Savannah: *The Elegant Steam Ship.* Athens: University of Georgia Press, 1963.

———. *"World's Greatest Ship": The Story of the* Leviathan. 4 vols. New York: South Street Seaport Museum, 1972–78.

Brinnin, J. M. *The Sway of the Grand Saloon: A Social History of the North Atlantic.* New York: Delacorte Press, 1971.

Brown, A. C. *Women and Children Last: The Tragic Loss of the Steamship* Arctic. Warwick, VA: Ballymena, 1954.

Bushell, T. A. *Royal Mail: A Centenary History of the Royal Mail Line, 1839–1939.* London: Trade and Travel Publications, 1939.

Cairis, N. T. *North Atlantic Passenger Liners Since 1900.* London: Ian Allan, 1972.

Cary, A. L. *Famous Liners and Their Stories.* New York: D. Appleton-Century Co., 1937.

———. *Giant Liners of the World.* London: S. Low, Marston & Co., 1930.

———. *Liners of the Ocean Highway.* London: S. Low, Marston & Co., n.d.

———. *Mail Liners of the World.* London: S. Low, Marston & Co., n.d.

Chadwick, F. E.; Kelley, J. D. J.; Hunt, R.; Gould, J. H.; Rideing, W. H.; and Seaton, A. E. *Ocean Steamships: A Popular Account of Their Construction, Development, Management and Appliances.* New York: C. Scribner's Sons, 1891.

Corson, F. R. *The Atlantic Ferry in the Twentieth Century.* London: S. Low, Marston & Co., n.d.

The Cunard Line. London: Electrotype Co., 1894.

DeBoer, M. G. *The Holland-America Line, 1873–1923.* Rotterdam: Holland-America Line, 1923.

DeGroot, F. A. B., ed. *The Ocean Express* Bremen. Munich: F. Bruckmann, n.d.

Dickens, C. *American Notes.* Gloucester, MA: Peter Smith, 1968.

Dodman, F. E. *Ships of the Cunard Line.* London: A. Coles, 1955.

Dowden, P. *Ships of the Royal Mail Lines.* London: A. Coles, 1954.

Droste, C. L., comp. *The* Lusitania *Case: Documents on the War.* Edited by W. H. Tantum IV. Riverside, CT: 7 C's Press, 1972.

Dugan, J. *The Great Iron Ship.* New York: Harper, 1953.

Duncan, W. J. *RMS* Queen Mary: *Queen of the Queens.* Anderson, SC: Droke House, 1969.

Dunn, L. *Passenger Liners.* 2d rev. ed. London: A. Coles, 1965.

Dunnett, A. M. *The Donaldson Line: A Century of Shipping, 1854–1954.* Glasgow: Jackson, Son & Co., 1960.

Emmerson, G. S. *The Greatest Iron Ship: S.S.* Great Eastern. North Pomfret, VT: David & Charles, n.d.

Farr, G. E. *The Steamship* Great Britain. Bristol: Bristol Branch of the Historical Association, 1965.

———. *The Steamship* Great Western: *The First Atlantic Liner.* Dursley, England: F. Bailey & Son, n.d.

Fry, H. *The History of North Atlantic Steam Navigation, with Some Account of Early Ships and Shipowners.* London: S. Low, Marston & Co., 1896.

Gregor, H. *The S.S.* Great Britain. New York: Macmillan Press, 1971.

History of the Anchor Line, 1852–1911. Glasgow: J. Horn, 1911.

Hoehling, A. A., and Hoehling, M. *The Last Voyage of the* Lusitania. London: Longmans, Green & Co., 1957.

Hughes, T. *The Blue Riband of the Atlantic.* New York: Charles Scribner's Sons, 1973.

The Lloyd Triestino: Notes and Remembrances, 1836–1920. Trieste: Instituto Italiano d'Arti Grafiche, 1920.

Maddocks, M. *The Great Liners.* Alexandria, VA: Time-Life Books, 1978.

Maginnis, A. J. *The Atlantic Ferry: Its Ships, Men, and Workings.* 3rd rev. ed. London: Whittaker & Co., 1900.

Maxtone-Graham, J. *The Only Way to Cross.* New York: Macmillan, 1972.

Oldham, W. J. *The Ismay Line, the White Star Line, and the Ismay Family Story.* Liverpool: Journal of Commerce, 1961.

Official Guide and Album of the Cunard Steamship Company. Rev. ed. London: Sutton Sharpe & Co., 1877.

Parker, H., and Bowen, F. C. *Mail Passenger Steamships of the Nineteenth Century.* Philadelphia: J.B. Lippincott Co., n.d.

Pond, E. L. R. *Junius Smith: Pioneer Promoter of Transatlantic Steam Navigation.* Mystic, CT: Marine Historical Association, 1941.

Potter, N., and Frost, J. *The* Queen Mary. New York: John Day Co., 1961.

Ransome-Wallis, P. *North Atlantic Panorama, 1900–1976.* Middletown, CT: Wesleyan Press, 1977.

Bibliography

Ridgely-Nevitt, C. *American Steamships on the Atlantic*. Newark: University of Delaware Press, 1981.

Seventy Years: North German Lloyd, Bremen, 1857–1927. Berlin: Atlantic-verlag, n.d.

Spratt, H. P. *One Hundred Years of Transatlantic Steam Navigation, 1838–1938*. London: His Majesty's Stationery Office, 1938.

———. *Outline History of Transatlantic Steam Navigation*. London: His Majesty's Stationery Office, 1950.

———. *Transatlantic Paddle Steamers*. 2d rev. ed. Glasgow: Brown, Son & Ferguson, 1967.

Staff, F. W. *The Transatlantic Mail*. London: A. Coles, 1956.

Tate, W. *Atlantic Conquest: The Men and Ships of the Glorious Age of Steam*. Boston: Little, Brown & Co., 1962.

Tyler, D. B. *Steam Conquers the Atlantic*. New York: D. Appleton-Century Co., 1939.

Vea, E.; Schreiner, J.; and Seland, J. *Den Norske Americkalinje, 1910–1960*. Oslo: Grondahl, 1960.

Wentholt, A. C. *Brug over den oceaan: Een eeuw geschiedenis van de Holland Amerika Lijn*. Rotterdam: Nijgh & Van Ditmar, 1973.

White, A. G. H. *Ships of the North Atlantic*. London: S. Low, Marston & Co., 1938.

The White Star Line of Mail Steamers. London: Ismay, Imrie & Co., 1877.

Wilson, V. S. F. *The Largest Ships of the World*. 2d rev. ed. London: C. Lockwood & Son, 1928.

Woon, B. D. *The Frantic Atlantic: An Intimate Guide to the Well-Known Deep*. London: A. A. Knopf, 1927.

Flags, Funnels & Ship Identification

Dunn, L. *Liners and Their Recognition*. New York: J. de Graff, 1953.

Granville, A., ed. *Transatlantic and Coastwise Steamship Funnel Marks, House-Flags and Night-Flags*. 2d annual ed. New York: Pelletreau & Raynor, 1875.

Pain, H. J., comp. *Distinguishing Night Signals of European and American Steamship Lines and Governments*. New York: C. F. Bloom, 1898.

Stewart, C. *Flags, Funnels, and Hull Colours*. New rev. ed. London: A. Coles, 1963.

Talbot-Booth, E. C., ed. *House-Flags & Funnels of British and Foreign Shipping Companies*. New York: D. Appleton-Century Co., 1937.

United States Hydrographic Office. *Merchant Marine House Flags and Stack Insignia*. Washington, D.C.: Hydrographic Office, 1961.

Wedge, F. J. N., comp. *Brown's Flags and Funnels of British and Foreign Steamship Companies*. Glasgow: Brown, Son & Ferguson, 1951.

Immigration and Emigration

Morris, J. M. *Our Maritime Heritage: Maritime Developments and Their Impact on American Life*. Washington, D.C.: University Press of America, 1979.

Morton Allen Directory of European Passenger Arrivals for the Years 1890 to 1930 at the Port of New York and for the Years 1904 to 1926 at the Ports of New York, Philadelphia and Baltimore. New York: Immigration Information Bureau, 1931.

Stevenson, R. L. *The Amateur Emigrant*. New York: C. Scribner's Sons, 1923.

Taylor, P. *The Distant Magnet: European Emigration to the U.S.A.* New York: Harper Torchbooks, 1971.

Marine Steam Technology

Baker, W. A. *The Engine Powered Vessel: From Paddle Wheeler to Nuclear Ship*. New York: Grosset & Dunlap, 1965.

Bauer, G. *Marine Engines and Boilers: Their Design and Construction*. Translated from the 2d German ed. by E. M. Donkin and S. B. Donkin. Edited by L. S. Robertson. New York: N. W. Henley Publishing Co., 1918.

Bourne, C. E. *A Treatise on the Screw Propeller*. 2d rev. ed. London: Longman, Brown, Green, & Longmans, 1855.

Bragg, E. M. *The Design of Marine Engines and Auxiliaries*. 2d rev. ed. New York: D. Van Nostrand Co., 1918.

Bibliography

Brown, A. C. *Twin Ships: Notes on the Chronological History of the Use of Multiple Hulled Vessels.* Newport News, VA: Mariners Museum, 1939.

Buchanan, R. *A Practical Treatise on Propelling Vessels by Steam.* London: R. Ackerman, 1816.

Donaldson, J. *The Practical Guide to the Use of Marine Steam Machinery and Internal Management of Small Steamers, Steam Yachts, and Steam Launches.* London: Norie & Wilson, 1885.

Ewing, J. A. *The Steam-Engine and Other Heat-Engines.* 2d rev. ed. Cambridge: University Press, 1899.

Gray, J. *Practical Single-Ended and Double-Ended Boilers.* London: Constable & Co., 1912.

Latrobe, J. H. B. *A Lost Chapter in the History of the Steamboat.* Baltimore: Maryland Historical Society, 1871.

Lucas, T.; Graham, F. D.; and Hawkins, N. *Audel's New Marine Engineers' Guide.* New York: T. Audel & Co., 1918.

Lyon, F., and Hinds, A. W. *Marine and Naval Boilers.* 2d rev. ed. Annapolis: United States Naval Institute, 1918.

Main, T. J., and Brown, T. *The Marine Steam-Engine.* 4th rev. ed. Philadelphia: H. C. Baird, 1864.

Marine Steam. New York: The Babcock & Wilcox Co., 1928.

Paget-Tomlinson, E. W. *Illustrated Handbook and Guide to the Steam Marine Engines.* 2d rev. ed. Liverpool: Liverpool City Museums, 1962.

Peabody, C. H., and Miller, E. F. *Steamboilers.* New York: J. Wiley & Sons, 1905.

Russell, J. S. *On the Nature, Properties, and Applications of Steam and on Steam Navigation.* Edinburgh: A. & C. Black, 1841.

Sennett, R., and Oram, H. J. *The Marine Steam Engine.* London: Longmans, Green & Co., 1918.

Sothern, J. W. M. *The Marine Steam Turbine.* 4th rev. ed. New York: D. Van Nostrand, 1916.

Stromeyer, J. P. E. C. *Marine Boiler Management and Construction.* 5th rev. ed. London: Longmans, Green & Co., 1919.

INDEX

Index